Haynes
Computer
Manual

© Haynes Publishing 2004

First published 2001
Revised 2nd edition 2002
Reprinted 2003
Revised 3rd edition 2004

Published by: Haynes Publishing
Sparkford, Yeovil, Somerset BA22 7JJ
Tel: 01063 442030 Fax: 01963 440001
Int. tel: +44 1963 442030 Fax: +44 1963 440001
E-mail: sales@haynes.co.uk
Web site: www.haynes.co.uk

British Library Cataloguing in Publication Data:
A catalogue record for this book is available from the British Library

ISBN 1 84425 128 4

Printed in Britain by J. H. Haynes & Co. Ltd., Sparkford

Haynes
Computer
Manual

The step-by-step guide to upgrading, repairing and maintaining a PC

Haynes Publishing

Contents

Introduction

Let's begin by asking two questions. Do you consider your home desktop computer system to be a fabulously powerful, immensely flexible, wholly essential and user-friendly tool? Or do you regard it as an overly complex, befuddling contraption, riddled with conflicting standards, prone to break down in any number of bizarre ways, instantly obsolete and bedevilled with an incomprehensible jargon developed by, and for, fully-fledged geeks?

Your answer to both questions is probably 'yes'. That's where we come in.

If you enjoy using your computer and want to make the most of your hardware (and your money) without becoming a dyed-in-the-wool techie in the process, this is the book for you. We'll show you in a series of clear step-by-step guides just how to upgrade, improve and enhance your system. We'll also consider how best to trouble-shoot problems and keep it all running smoothly. Above all, we'll endeavour to make everything easy.

Do please remember one thing: a computer is not like this year's model of a particular make of car. It's simply not possible for us to predict with any degree of certainty what's sitting on your desktop. Quite the reverse, in fact. The very essence and, indeed, appeal of the personal computer is that one size resolutely does not suit all: you can make of your system just what you will. This inevitably means that there are limitations to what we can cover here, and so our approach throughout is to focus on the most likely and common configurations.

The alternative – and there is only one – is to try to cover all angles, all bases, all permutations, all possible problems. What you end up with then is a massively unwieldy tome that ties itself in knots with cross-references and tables and endless ifs and buts … and still doesn't succeed in its aims.

No, we've striven instead to cover the basics and to give you enough background knowledge to tackle your own computer setup with confidence.

To that end, we're making certain assumptions here.

First, about you:

You have a working (although not necessarily thorough) knowledge of Windows

You don't have an unlimited budget (or else you'd buy a brand new computer every six months and stay ahead of the game)

You're not scared to perform minor surgery on your computer (but you'd rather know what you're doing than fumble in the dark).

And secondly, about your computer:

It has an Intel Pentium/Celeron II, III or 4 processor or the AMD Athlon/Duron equivalent

It's running Windows 98, Millennium Edition or XP

It dates back no further than 1997–8 (any older and you really should be thinking about a replacement)

It's a PC, not a Mac!

Just a word on that last comment. Mac users are a sorely overlooked species in much computer literature. True, there aren't that many of them around, relatively speaking, despite the popular iMac and Power Mac ranges, but that's no excuse. The real point is that a Mac has quite a different architecture to a PC and a significantly different operating system, and it's simply impractical, unhelpful and ultimately unfair to stick in the odd 'oh, and if you have a Mac, you might want to try this…' section in a book that deals primarily with PCs. That is why we wrote a separate manual specifically for Mac users, entitled *The Haynes Mac Manual*. This, then, is the manual for the discerning but probably somewhat frustrated owner of an 'average' Windows-based Pentium-powered PC. We can't promise to turn it into a supercomputer overnight but we certainly hope to help you prolong its lifespan and/or make it significantly better. We keep the jargon to a minimum and practical guidance to the fore. After all, reading about computers is probably not high on your list of priorities and upgrading, repairing and maintaining your hardware is not, with the best will in the world, what you might call fun. But using your computer should be fun and that's the point of this manual: to help ensure that your PC serves you well both now and in the future, however your needs may change.

How to use this book

 Single click on the left mouse button

 Double click on the left mouse button

 Single click on the right mouse button

 Check or uncheck this option by clicking the left mouse button

 Type the following text on your keyboard

In the text, consecutive directions are sometimes expressed as e.g. Click Start > Programs > Accessories. The > symbol means 'followed by'. Wherever possible, we illustrate actions with screenshots and describe them in the text.

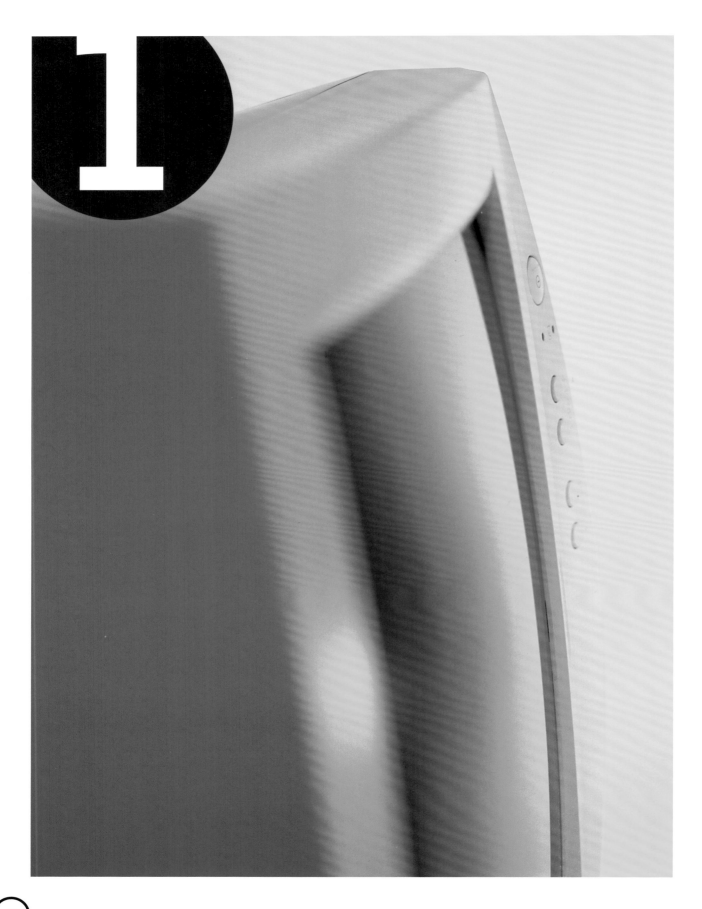

1

PART 1

Getting to know your PC

First things first. Before we start poking around under the hood, let's take stock of your current computer setup. We're not exactly doing rocket science here but the best place to start is undoubtedly with a little basic background knowledge.

PART

A brief history of personal computing

It has become something of a cliché to say that the Apollo moon missions were managed with less computing power than you'll find in today's typical car, electronic organiser, digital watch or musical greetings card... but it illustrates the pace of progress well. These days, everything from your kettle to your key ring carries a microchip and that bland, beige box perched on your desktop is capable of performing more calculations in a split second than any mere mortal could achieve in a hundred lifetimes.

But it's a mistake to allow yourself to be overawed by technology. Always remember that a computer is a tool – no more and no less. It may be faster but you're smarter. (No, honestly, you are.) The chances are that you'll never really understand how your computer works, but so what? What counts is understanding how all the various bits and pieces work together. Grasp that and you'll soon be stripping, upgrading and rebuilding your PC before breakfast.

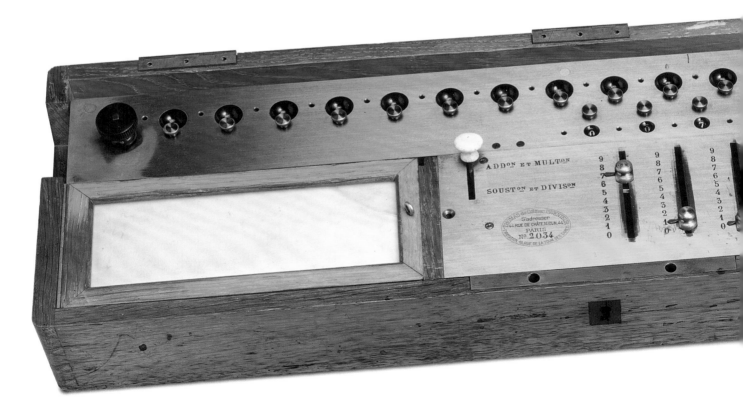

A functioning computer is essentially comprised of three parts

Hardware: *the motherboard, memory, processor, monitor, keyboard, modem, mouse and all the other nuts and bolts.*

Operating system: *the master program that makes the hardware and software work together in perfect harmony (usually).*

Application software: *programs that let you do useful things with your PC such as write letters, perform calculations, surf the internet and much, much more.*

If you can get the distinction between hardware, the operating system and application software clear in your mind from the outset, then you've overcome one major hurdle. Not that it's altogether straightforward, mind: Microsoft Windows infamously blurs the lines between software required to run a computer and extras that make life easier for the user and/or stifle commercial competition. Anyway, if for now you don't know Windows from Word, ROM from RAM or a chipset from a chipolata, don't panic. You will, we promise.

So just how did we get here? Well, ask any two specialists about what really matters in the story of computing and you'll likely get two very different answers. But the one thing that they – and we – will agree upon is this: despite the chequered, convoluted and complex evolution of the personal computer, these days just about anybody can get to grips with the technology. What was once the exclusive province of boffins is now familiar territory to millions.

And that's a good thing. All you need is a little patience, a dash of logic, the confidence to tinker – and, of course, this manual as your guide.

Charles X Thomas de Colmar invented his Arithmometer in 1820. It was the first commercially successful calculating machine and could be used for addition, subtraction, division and multiplication.

A controversial timeline

500BC   Ernie the Egyptian invents the abacus. Blame him

1642   Blaise Pascal invents an automatic adding machine of sorts

1674   Gottfried von Leibniz upgrades the Pascaline by adding multiplication

1822   Charles Babbage designs his Difference Engine, a mechanical calculator, but can't raise sufficient venture capital to build it

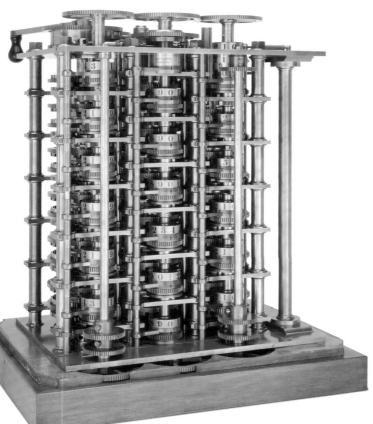

Right: A Chinese Abacus, the Suan Pan is the oldest form of abacus still in use.

Below: Charles Babbage's Difference engine was finished in 1822. It was a decimal digital machine.

1833   Babbage upgrades his earlier invention to an Analytical Engine but doesn't build this one either

1890   Herman Hollerith comes up with a method for using punched cards to store data

1911   The Computing-Tabulating-Recording Company is founded in New York, and soon becomes IBM (International Business Machines)

1939   John Vincent Atanasoff and Clifford Berry invent the first true digital computer

1943   Alan Turing invents the *other* first true digital computer, Colossus, and uses it to crack the Germans' wartime Enigma code

1946   John Presper Eckert and John Mauchly develop ENIAC (Electronic Numerical Integrator And Computer), a fully-fledged computer replete with processor. It weighed in at 30 tonnes

1951   Eckert and Mauchly unveil UNIVAC (Universal Automatic Computer), the first computer to be sold commercially on the high street. It cost around $5m

1958   IBM develops a computer that uses transistors instead of valves

1964   The integrated circuit is used for the first time in computer design

1965   Digital Equipment Corporation launches the first minicomputer, the PDP-8

1969   The US Department of Defense sets up a computer network called ARPANet (Advanced Research Projects Agency) that will one day become the internet

1970   The UNIX operating system is developed. So is the 8 inch floppy disk

1973   The first hard disk arrives courtesy of IBM: a 30MB tiddler called Winchester

1975   The Altair 8800 – the first microcomputer, or PC – is sold to the public. It cost $400 and you had to build it yourself. Bill Gates and Paul Allen found Microsoft

1976   Steve Jobs and Steve Wozniak found Apple Computer

1978   The 5.25 inch floppy disk becomes the (temporary) standard medium for portable, removable storage

1980   British inventor Clive Sinclair launches the kit-form ZX-80 computer. Sales of soldering irons soar and a generation of geeks is born. It cost £79.95 plus £8.95 for the power supply. Ready-assembled model launched a month later at £99.95 to wicked and unsubstantiated rumours that they were customer-assembled models returned to Sinclair for repair

The large disk is from an IBM system of 1984 and can hold 4MB, compared with the small hard disk from 1999 which can hold 6GB!

The Altair 8800b microcomputer of 1975.

'PalmPilot' palmtop computer of 1998. Manufactured by US Robotics.

1981	The IBM PC hits the streets at £3000 and Acorn releases the popular BBC Micro. The 3.5 inch floppy disk also makes its first appearance
1982	The PC wins Time Magazine's 'Man of the Year' and the Sinclair ZX Spectrum brings computer games to the mass market
1984	Apple introduces the Macintosh computer. It uses a mouse and clickable icons and menus
1985	The first commercial version of Windows is launched by Microsoft
1988	Apple sues Microsoft for copying the graphical look and feel of its operating system. Then again, Apple allegedly pinched the idea from Xerox
1991	Tim Berners-Lee invents the World Wide Web. Life is never quite the same again
1994	Jeff Bozos quits Wall Street and decides to start an internet bookstore, Amazon.com
1995	Microsoft introduces Windows 95, which looks suspiciously like the Apple Mac. People suddenly find PCs easy to use, sales skyrocket, and Bill Gates becomes rather rich
1996	Microsoft introduces Internet Explorer and sets off a browser war with Netscape, ultimately making web browsing software free
1999	Internet businesses become the hottest stocks around the world. Millionaires are created as fast as you can say IPO
2000	The great dotcom crash! Reality kicks in and web businesses go to the wall in droves
2001	In the wake of the crash, PC and peripheral prices fall, making computer hardware the best buy ever
2002	Processors are now well into the 2GHz-plus range, i.e. capable of performing over two billion calculations per second
2003	Worms and viruses hit the headlines and make computing temporarily miserable for all affected. The Recording Industry Association of America sues a bunch of file swappers. Weblogs make a mark
2004	Google floats and heralds the start of Dotcom Boom Madness Part 2, Microsoft patches the millionth hole in Windows, processor speeds top 3GHz and defy the laws of physics, PCs finally make it into the living room in the guise of home entertainment centres, and Ernie the Egyptian spins in his sarcophagus with the excitement of it all. Now let's get to work…

PART

Why upgrade?

Back in 1965, a rising young engineer called Gordon Moore who went on to co-found Intel noted that computers had a habit of doubling in power every 18 months or so. His observation came to be enshrined as 'Moore's Law' and, remarkably, still holds true today (although physical constraints on the complexity of processor circuits are beginning to threaten it). Ironically, we long ago passed the point where we actually need more computing power in our homes and offices, and yet still we rush lemming-like to upgrade or replace hardware that's barely out of warranty. Why?

Because I can? No, no, no… that's the answer of an inveterate geek. Now there's nothing wrong with being an inveterate geek – well, okay, there is, but we won't go into that here – but if you're the type to fix things that positively ain't broke, this ain't the book for you.

Because I want to? *Really?* You get kicks from tinkering with hardware? Really? There's certainly much satisfaction to be had from fixing or improving a PC but we'd draw the line at calling it fun.

Because I must? Absolutely. This is the only time when it makes true sense to upgrade your PC. There are, in fact, three distinct but related good reasons to upgrade.

Three good reasons to upgrade

To improve performance This is when your existing setup simply isn't up to the demands placed upon it, often as a result of changes in your own work or play habits. A system purchased to look after the accounts is unlikely to cut the mustard at 3-D gaming.

While performance-enhancing upgrades can significantly prolong the lifespan of your PC, it's important to make the right upgrades. As we go along, we'll consider which upgrades are practicable and worthwhile – and when it's better to admit defeat, throw the whole system in the skip and start afresh with a brand new computer!

To repair a broken component Unfortunately, unless you're a dab hand with a soldering iron, your chances of actually repairing anything are slim indeed. You could take a can opener to a stalled hard disk or hotwire a sound card... but we wouldn't recommend it. No, the fact is that when something breaks down, it almost always need replacing – and in such cases it's easy to make a virtue of necessity by installing something altogether better. Why replace an ancient, slow CD-ROM drive with like for like when you could just as easily fit a shiny new recordable DVD drive? True, if you want to make your own movies, you might need a memory upgrade as well, and perhaps even a faster processor – which takes us back to improving performance.

To add new features Need a backup device? Run out of hard disk space? Fancy a bigger, flatter, lighter monitor or a better printer? Want to edit images from your digital camera? How about

Boosting, repairing and enhancing a PC are all good reasons for minor surgery.

adding a hub to hook up two or more PCs in a home network? These are examples of upgrading a system by adding things that are currently lacking – as indeed would be adding a recordable DVD drive to replace or complement a CD drive. Again, we'll look at all the main options.

But before we get carried away, let's consider two further questions

Do you need really *need* to upgrade? Please understand that we're not trying to discourage you from upgrading your PC – quite the reverse – but there are times when a little sober reflection can pay dividends and save you money. For instance, is your software placing unnecessary demands on your hardware? Do you really need that full-blown, memory-hogging monolithic office suite just to balance the household budget? Would it be worthwhile buying a dedicated games console instead of converting your dusty old computer to a lean, mean fighting/driving/flying machine? Is your hard disk clogged with seldom-used programs that could easily be deleted to free up space? And would simply defragmenting your hard disk make a world of difference to your PC's performance?

If much of this sounds deeply mysterious right now, read on: we'll cover all the angles in detail soon enough. But if you're contemplating an upgrade simply because your once fleet-of-foot system is now limping lamely, jump straight to the Maintenance section in Part Seven. A little rudimentary housekeeping can work wonders – and save you a packet.

***Can* you upgrade?** The ongoing trend in computer design is to integrate as many features as possible on the central circuit board, or motherboard, rather than relying on hardware expansion cards. A computer with an integrated graphics chip and audio chip is cheaper to make and sell than one kitted out with separate graphics and sound cards. It also means that PCs can become smaller, less power-hungry and consequently quieter. However, this trend has one unfortunate downside, which is that it becomes tricky to upgrade to more powerful graphics or sound cards later.

Similar thinking dictates that outmoded 'legacy' interfaces should be swept aside in favour of cheaper, more reliable machines that can be expanded indefinitely through USB and FireWire ports. Again, however, this can render older but still serviceable peripherals obsolete. Many a printer with a parallel port has found itself unemployed when the new PC arrives sans suitable interface. If your PC is relatively recent, you may find that your upgrade options are hampered by design. This will become evident when we lift the lid and look inside. The good news is that there are almost always workarounds, and we'll mention these as we go through.

One day, perhaps, PCs will be ten a penny and it'll be cheaper to buy a new one than fuss around with upgrades and repairs. One day, perhaps, PCs will be genuinely easy to use. And one day, just perhaps, the PC will cease to exist in anything like its current shape and form.

But not today, and probably not tomorrow. For now, millions of us own computer systems that are teetering on the edge of obsolescence but are not quite ready for the skip. This is the manual for people who can use a screwdriver but not a soldering iron; people who won't throw good money after bad but don't want to buy a new computer unless and until they absolutely have to; and people who are allergic to acronyms.

When a computer is this cute, motherboard integration is the key and expansion card slots are in short supply.

PART **1** **Outside explained**

DVD-ROM (Read-Only Memory) drive *DVD drives read discs that look similar to CDs but have a much great storage capacity. DVD-ROM drives can also play movie discs, which effectively turns your PC into a DVD player or home cinema. Recordable DVD drives – that is, drives that let you copy files or films onto blank DVD discs – are now becoming the norm and certainly make an attractive upgrade option, as we shall see. All DVD drives can read or play CDs, and most recordable DVD drives can also record CDs.*

CD-ROM/CD-RW drive *A compact disc player that reads multimedia and audio CDs, equally suited to installing software and playing music. CD-ROM drives can read, or play, CDs but a CD-RW (Rewriteable) drive lets you make your own from files on your computer, including music and video. This makes it ideal for backing up important files and for making your own audio CDs that can be played in any CD player. You may find that your computer has a 'combo' CD-RW and DVD-ROM drive.*

On/off switch *Does just what you'd expect. Of course, you know better than to switch off a PC without first going through the proper Windows shut down procedure, don't you (bizarre though it may be to press a Start button to stop the operating system)?*

Floppy drive *Floppy disks are a stalwart form of removable media. But while they may be cheap, the drives are sluggish and capacity is limited to 1.44MB per disk. We'll look at a more flexible alternative later (see p84).*

Power LED *This light lets you know that your computer is switched on, just in case the fan wasn't loud enough to clue you in.*

Drive activity LED *A light that flashes when the computer is busy reading or writing data from or to the hard disk. For information only.*

Reset switch *When Windows freezes and all else fails, this button restarts the system. Not one to push in error.*

Case *The majority of PCs now come in tower format (tall and narrow) rather than desktop (flat and wide). There are various standards governing case design, related to the size and shape of the motherboard within. The current trend is to integrate as many features on the motherboard as possible, which makes it possible for PCs to be squeezed into ever-smaller cases. Many of the latest 'Media Center' models actually look more like DVD players than computers.*

Interface All this talk of ports and sockets and connectors may sound baffling – and, let's be honest, you couldn't contrive to concoct a more counter-intuitive, jargon-riddled language if you tried – but keep in mind that these are just different types of interface. An interface, of course, is just a way of connecting two bits of kit and getting them talking to each other. It would be easier if everything used the same interface, but then you wouldn't need this manual. See Appendix 2 for a close-up guide to common connectors.

Power socket A three-pin power cable plugs in here to connect your computer to the mains electricity.

Power switch If present (don't worry if it's not), this switch controls the internal power supply. As a rule, you would leave this switch at the on position and use the on/off switch on the front of the case to turn on the PC.

PS/2-type ports 6-pin female sockets, one for the mouse and one for the keyboard. These are generally colour-coded green and purple respectively. The current trend is for both keyboard and mouse to use USB sockets instead, or to go cordless and 'talk' to the computer via radio waves.

USB ports Newer sockets generally not found on PCs built before 1997–8. Faster and more flexible·than either parallel or serial ports, USB (Universal Serial Bus) is now the de facto standard for connecting external devices.

Audio connectors A PC fitted with a sound card will typically have one or two outlets for speakers and jacks for connecting a microphone and other audio equipment. It may also have a game port designed for a joystick. This example is unusual because it features both built-in sound capabilities (top) and a separate sound card (bottom). The built-in circuitry has been disabled to allow the more powerful sound card to run the show.

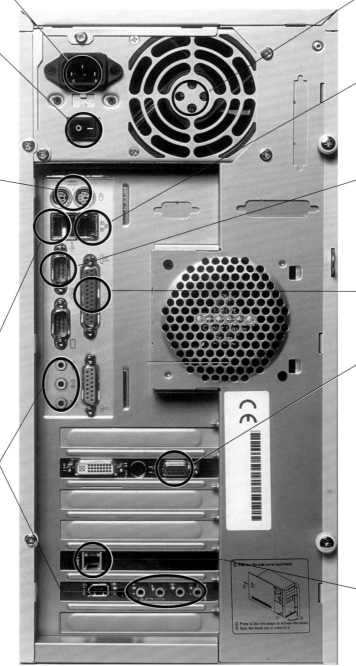

Cooling fan Air inlet for the internal fan. Without suitable cooling, a PC would soon get hot enough to fry an egg. And its own circuitry.

Ethernet connector If the PC is equipped to be connected to a network, there will be an 8-pin RJ-45 socket for connecting it to a hub or directly to another computer.

Serial port A 9-pin male socket commonly used to connect external modems and older mice. Two such ports are the norm, known to Windows as COM1 and COM2. Virtually obsolete.

Parallel port A 25-pin female socket commonly used to connect a printer. Windows refers to this port as LPT1.

Monitor connector A 15-pin female VGA socket used to connect the monitor. This is the visible end of the internal graphics card. Depending upon the capabilities of the card, there may also be an array of video outputs. Here we see an S-video TV-out port (black, round) for broadcasting a signal to a television set and also a digital connector (white, rectangular) for use with the very latest digital LCD monitors.

Modem connector If the PC has an internal modem, there will be a 6-pin RJ-11 socket to connect it to the telephone system via a cable.

PART  # Inside explained

We don't suggest for a minute that you dive straight to the innards of your PC but we're going to be talking a lot about motherboards, components and expansion cards as we go on. Here's a sneak preview of what to expect under the hood.

Power supply *A metal-cased assembly that converts AC utility power into the special low current voltages required by your computer.*

Processor *Usually thought of as the brains of a computer, the processor does number crunching on a grand scale. Chances are you'll have either an Intel or an AMD processor onboard, sitting either in a socket mounting (flat on the motherboard) or in a slot (on edge). You won't actually see a socketed processor because there will be a fan unit bolted on top keeping it cool.*

Graphics card *The graphics card is a printed circuit board responsible for producing the images that you see on your monitor screen. It's possible to build the circuitry right into the motherboard but this is an example of an expansion card (discussed in detail on p90).*

Free expansion slots *These are motherboard interfaces into which you plug circuit boards to add new features to your computer. A sound card is merely one example of many possibilities.*

Sound card *An expansion card that provides the PC with audio capabilities. Note the cable linking the sound card to the CD-ROM drive. This enables the card to pick up the soundtrack on an audio CD or CD-ROM and broadcast it through speakers or headphones.*

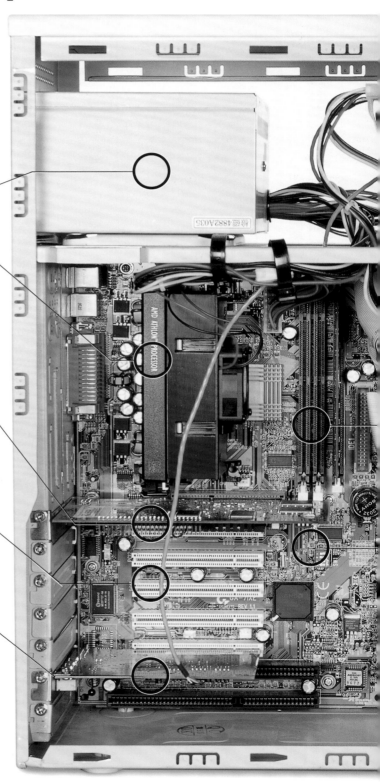

CD-ROM drive

Floppy drive

Hard disk *The hard disk is a device that permanently stores data until such time as you decide to delete or modify it. Every time you hit the Save button in a word processor, for instance, the document you're working on is copied to the hard disk, so it's safe even if the power is suddenly switched off. The process of saving data is called writing to the hard disk; retrieving it is reading from the hard disk.*

Memory *Random Access Memory, or RAM, comes in sticks called memory modules that sit in slots on the motherboard. RAM is a temporary working space in which the PC's business is conducted from moment to moment. The more you have, the more you things you can do simultaneously (a.k.a. multitasking).*

Motherboard *A great big printed circuit board. You really can't miss it because everything else plugs into it one way or another. Think of it as your PC's nervous system – a series of channels and conduits transmitting information from any one part of the system to any other. Getting hold of the manual that came with your motherboard is going to save a lot of headaches and uncertainty later.*

TECHIE CORNER

Drive Bays A drive bay is a space in the case into which a drive may be installed. For reasons too dull to discuss, two sizes evolved, as shown here. Floppy and hard disk drives use the 3.5-inch standard and virtually everything else the 5.25-inch standard. Note that the latter is also referred to as a half-height drive, so don't panic if you come across the term.

Drive bay	3.5"	5.25"
Actual width	4"	5.75"
Actual depth	5.75"	8"
Actual height	1"	1.63"

PART **1**

Peripherals explained

The items on these pages are examples of what are commonly referred to as peripherals. You may be surprised to find the monitor comes under this heading – after all, you can't do much with a PC without one – but the hard disk is also, strictly speaking, a peripheral device. That is, a computer is still technically a computer without a storage device, a display unit or input devices. What it patently is not is useful! That's where peripherals come in: they let you do exciting, fun, useful stuff with your computer.

Speakers *These range from cheap, tinny and worthless to quite extraordinarily powerful. Speakers either plug directly into the sound card or, if you have a surround sound setup, into a separate amplifier or subwoofer. Here, the subwoofer is the big black square box.*

Mouse *Small plastic clickable rodent that lives on a mat. The premiere pointing device, the mouse allows you to issue commands and move objects without typing.*

Keyboard *A dumb typewriter renowned for accumulating crumbs and other debris. It translates the motion of your fingers pressing keys into digital codes that your computer interprets as numbers, letters, and commands.*

TECHIE CORNER

Peripherals It's possible to add no end of peripheral devices to a computer. Indeed, it's this very expandability that makes the PC such a flexible tool. A webcam, for instance, lets you make face-to-face calls to family overseas via the internet; a graphics tablet turns a computer into a digital easel; and a MIDI keyboard opens up all manner of musical possibilities.

Webcam.

Graphics tablet.

MIDI keyboard.

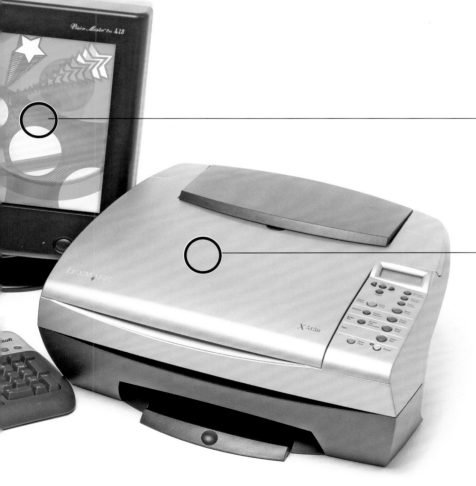

Monitor A display screen housed within a big, deep, bulky box – or, if it's modern, a smaller, flatter, sleeker box.

Scanner Scanners take digital pictures of documents or printed photographs. You can then view, edit and print these images on the PC. Optional but rather useful. Here, the printer and scanner have been integrated in the same box, imaginatively known as a multi-function device (MFD).

Printer Despite the dream of a paperless office, hard copies of documents still have a place in most of our lives. The printer turns your computer's output into hard copy, nowadays with photo-realistic colour and near-professional quality levels.

PART

Taking stock

If you've ever bought off-the-shelf software, you'll know that there's usually a panel on the box stating the 'minimum system requirements'. Something along the lines of:

- **Intel Pentium II 266MHz** or better
- **Windows 98/Me/2000/XP**
- **64MB** of RAM (128MB recommended)
- **500MB** free hard disk space
- **CD-ROM** drive
- **Sound** card
- **Internet** connection

But what does it all mean? And does your PC come up to scratch? That's one issue; another crops up when you come to go shopping for upgrade components. You see, you can't just buy a bit more RAM without knowing what kind of RAM you need. And how much. And whether there's space for it on the motherboard.

The good news is if you start off with a thorough inventory of your current system, you really can't go far wrong. First of all, dig out the paperwork that came with your new PC. Here, you should find all the main specifications clearly laid out. However, that's only going to get you so far (and, of course, it's highly possible that you no longer have or simply can't find the original documentation). Thus we turn to Windows.

Check the minimum system requirements before you splash out on software.

Device advice
(Windows 98 and Millennium Edition)

Start.

Settings.

Control Panel.

System.

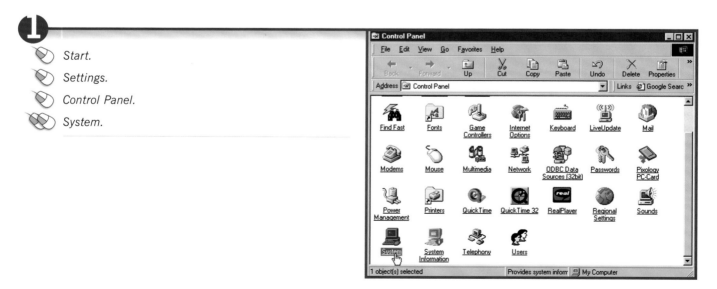

Device Manager tab

Now, just by using Device Manager, you can investigate your entire hardware setup at a glance. Click the + sign alongside any component to see more detail. In this example, we've expanded the CD-ROM section and can see that there are two drives installed (one made by Mitsumi, the other by Samsung).

General tab

Here you can see how much RAM is inside your PC – in this case, 256MB. We can also see that the processor is an AMD model.

 Start.

 Programs.

 Accessories.

 System Tools.

 System Information.

The System Information tool is another non-surgical route to the heart of your hardware. Again, click the + signs to see details of individual components. Windows 95 users can also use System Information but it may look rather different to this picture.

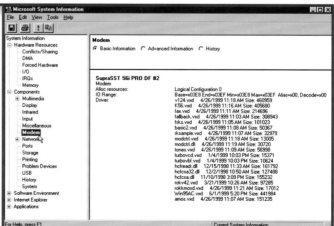

Device advice (Windows XP)

1

- Start
- Control Panel
- Performance and Maintenance
- System

In Windows XP, the click route is slightly different but the end result is similar. Device Manager is accessible from the Hardware tab. You can also get to this System Properties screen by right-clicking the My Computer icon on the Desktop and selecting properties from the popup menu.

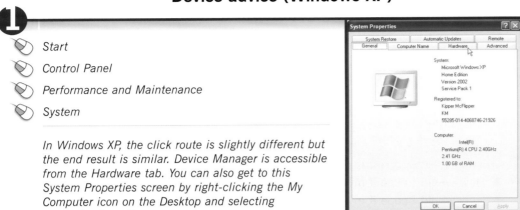

2

- Start.
- All Programs
- Accessories
- System Tools
- System Information.

Access System Information thus. A shorter route is to click Start > Run, then type 'msinfo32.exe' (without the quotes) and click OK.

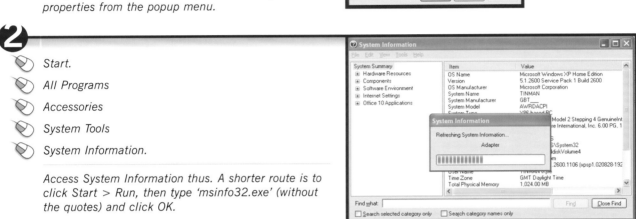

Digging deeper

If you want to check that your Pentium processor is ticking over at the correct clock speed, download and run the Intel Processor Frequency ID Utility. This is available from:
http://support.intel.com/support/processors/tools/frequencyid/download.htm
If you have an AMD Athlon processor, use the AMD CPUID utility: **www.amd.com/us-en/assets/content_type/utilities/amdcpuid.exe**

For more information than Windows alone provides – often much, much more – consider using third-party utility software (see p154). One of the best dedicated tools is Sandra (System ANalyser, Diagnostic and Reporting Assistant). A free Standard version is available from **www.sisoftware.co.uk/sandra** Its many tools will tell you just about everything you'll ever need to know about your system – hardware, software, technical configurations – and it's easier to use and clearer than Windows' own tools. The Professional version ($35 at the time of writing) has 80 separate modules that cover every base.

Also see the note on the Belarc Advisor software on p40.

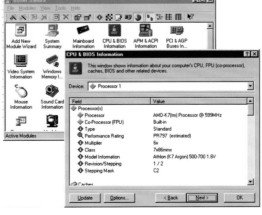

Software utilities let you see just what your system is made of.

PART 1

Taking precautions

Before turning another page, and certainly before taking a screwdriver to your computer, ask yourself these questions:

● How would I cope if my PC refuses to restart?
● How would I cope if my files become corrupted?
● How would I cope if my PC is stolen?

Temporary inconvenience or a major catastrophe? If your computer went badly awry, would you lose a day's work, week's work, or the sum total of your efforts over the past year?

Safe or sorry?

It's important to recognise the difference between a computer failure and the loss of data. In the case of a software problem, it's usually possible to reinstall Windows (and any of your programs that you need to) from scratch. Tedious, but possible, and with luck all your documents and files will survive. However, a better idea is to take precautionary measures now, and that means making a start-up disk. This way, you'll stand a good chance of fixing the problem from within. At the very least, you should be able to make emergency copies of your files.

Losing data is an altogether more serious proposition. No matter how careful you are, any computer upgrade, repair or maintenance carries with it a risk of damage. The only sensible approach – and believe us, we speak from hard and bitter experience – is to make backup copies of all your important files. In fact, make multiple copies, do it regularly, and keep them somewhere safe (and safe does not mean in your desk drawer: it means in an entirely different location, ideally in a fireproof box hidden under somebody else's floorboards!). There's a good chance that you made a Windows start-up disk (or rescue, emergency or boot disk – they're all one and the same thing) when you first bought or acquired your computer. There's a higher chance still that you've since misplaced it, so let's make a fresh one now. Just follow these step-by-step instructions.

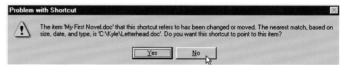

Lost files are at best a headache but can sometimes prove disastrous.

Making a Windows 98/Millennium Edition startup disk

1

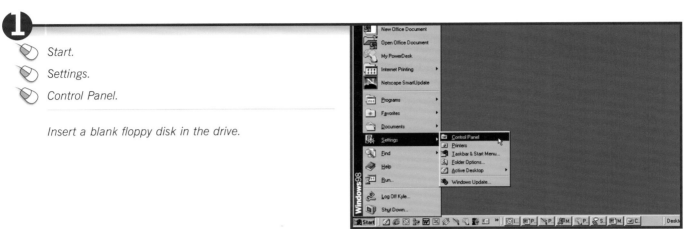

👆 *Start.*

👆 *Settings.*

👆 *Control Panel.*

Insert a blank floppy disk in the drive.

2

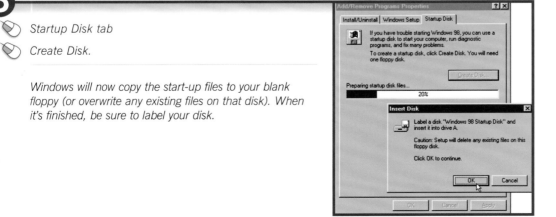

👆 *Add/Remove Programs*

It's not the most obvious route to making a start-up disk…

3

👆 *Startup Disk tab*

👆 *Create Disk.*

Windows will now copy the start-up files to your blank floppy (or overwrite any existing files on that disk). When it's finished, be sure to label your disk.

With support

Restart the computer with the start-up disk in its drive. Instead of seeing the familiar Windows screen – remember, this is for emergencies when Windows itself is in need of repair – the computer will stay in DOS mode and give you the option to start it up with or without CD-ROM support. Select the 'with support' option and note which drive letter is assigned to your CD drive (here it is E).

```
Preparing to start your computer.
This may take a few minutes. Please wait...

The diagnostic tools were successfully loaded to drive D.

MSCDEX Version 2.25
Copyright (C) Microsoft Corp. 1986-1995. All rights reserved.
        Drive E: = Driver MSCD001 unit 0

To get help, type HELP and press ENTER.

A:\
```

 e:

 dir

 Enter

When you see a blinking A:\> prompt, type the drive letter assigned to your CD drive. Now put any disc in the CD-ROM drive, type 'dir' and press the Enter key. If you can see a list of the files on the disk, congratulations. You could now reinstall Windows from the original CD-ROM.

```
E:\>dir

 Volume in drive E is WIN98
 Directory of E:\

ADD_ONS      <DIR>           04-23-99 10:22p
AUTORUN  INF        81       04-23-99 10:22p
CDSAMPLE     <DIR>           04-23-99 10:22p
DRIVERS      <DIR>           04-23-99 10:22p
README   TXT     3,096       04-23-99 10:22p
SETUP    EXE     3,824       04-23-99 10:22p
SETUPTIP TXT     3,646       04-23-99 10:22p
TOOLS        <DIR>           04-23-99 10:22p
WIN98        <DIR>           04-23-99 10:22p
         4 file(s)        10,647 bytes
         5 dir(s)             0 bytes free
```

setup.exe

We won't follow through on this but installing Windows is straightforward. Start the computer with the floppy as just described, put your Windows CD in the drive, follow the directions in Step 5 to access the CD directory, and start the Windows setup program by typing 'setup.exe'. Windows will now install, overwriting (deleting) the existing version in the process. Not something to do lightly.
In the meantime, remove the floppy disk from its drive and press the reset switch. Windows will now start as normal.

```
AUTORUN  INF        81       04-23-99 10:22p
CDSAMPLE     <DIR>           04-23-99 10:22p
DRIVERS      <DIR>           04-23-99 10:22p
README   TXT     3,096       04-23-99 10:22p
SETUP    EXE     3,824       04-23-99 10:22p
SETUPTIP TXT     3,646       04-23-99 10:22p
TOOLS        <DIR>           04-23-99 10:22p
WIN98        <DIR>           04-23-99 10:22p
         4 file(s)        10,647 bytes
         5 dir(s)             0 bytes free

E:\>setup.exe
Please wait while Setup initializes.

Setup is now going to perform a routine check on your system.

To continue, press ENTER. To quit Setup, press ESC.
```

Label your Windows start-up disk and keep it somewhere safe.

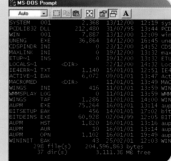

TECHIE CORNER

DOS or MS-DOS, or Microsoft Disk Operating System to be precise. This is a text-only operating system that came before Windows and is now largely irrelevant in daily PC use (praise be). However, DOS is still present on PCs running Windows 95 and 98, and it can prove invaluable when Windows refuses to work.

Making a Windows 95 startup disk

Oh dear. It all gets a bit messy now. The problem is that Windows 95 start-up disks do not include drivers for the CD-ROM drive. In other words, although the disk will start the system and allow you to carry out rudimentary repair work (if you know how), there's no way to access the CD-ROM drive. What this means is that you can't reinstall Windows because that requires access to, er, the CD-ROM drive. Not brilliant, is it?

The solution is to locate a DOS driver for your CD-ROM drive and include it on the start-up disk. If you're lucky, and if you've kept everything that shipped with the original equipment, you may find a floppy disk helpfully labelled 'This is a DOS driver for your CD-ROM drive'. But what are the chances of that happening? One approach is to establish who made the drive by looking in Device Manager, as described earlier. Make a note of the model. Now track down the company's website and look for a driver download area. Be sure to look for a DOS driver, not a Windows driver (which is quite different and useless in the present circumstances). Alternatively, try the following websites:

www.drivershq.com
www.driverzone.com

Once you have located and/or downloaded the appropriate driver, make a start-up disk as described above. The procedure may vary slightly depending upon which version of Windows 95 you have. When that's done, copy the DOS driver onto the floppy disk. Unfortunately, at this point you also have to manually edit some critical system files on the disk, and this is when it all gets horribly complicated. For the clearest walkthrough of the process, visit Bob O'Donnell's page here:

www.everythingcomputers.com/windows_boot_disk.htm

This site is also worth a visit, and it includes a file download to get your startup disk working with generic CD drives:
http://www.fixwindows.com/win95/cdboot.htm

Better still, upgrade to Windows 98, Millennium Edition or XP now and be done with this startup silliness!

...and why you don't have to with Windows XP

The Windows XP installation CD-ROM is itself bootable, which means you can use it to start the computer without resort to a floppy disk. Once up and running, you can use the Recovery Console to replace damaged files or otherwise effect a repair, or reinstall Windows completely (see p172). The only tweak you may need to make is configuring the BIOS to boot from the CD/DVD drive before the hard disk. See Appendix 1 for details.

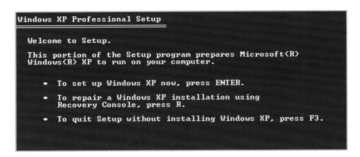

The Windows XP CD-ROM is bootable. Use it to start your computer and access the Recovery Console.

TECHIE CORNER

Driver A driver is a software program that enables your PC's operating system to communicate with a hardware device. Most upgrades involve installing drivers. Without one in place, the computer either won't realise that it's just grown a new limb or will recognise that *something* has been bolted on but can't do a thing with it. New drivers are often written throughout the lifespan of a device and it pays to check the manufacturer's website from time to time. An updated driver will often fix problems with an earlier version or even add new functionality.

Backing up your files

Quite how you make copies of your valuable files depends largely upon your system. That is, if you have nothing but a floppy drive onboard, you're pretty well limited to shifting data in batches of 1.44MB or less (which equates to around 700 disks per gigabyte!). Zip drives, by contrast, use disks with capacities of 100 or 250MB, depending on the model, but you don't see many of them around these days and the disks themselves have always been remarkably costly. A CD writer drive lets you back up 700MB of data at a time, and quickly too. A DVD offers even greater flexibility at 4.7GB – the equivalent of over three thousand floppies – and is all-but the norm today.

Indeed, one of the best reasons for upgrading a PC is to improve your options for backing up data.

Getting your backup

One method is simply to copy your files onto a floppy or Zip disk using Windows Explorer or My Computer. However, before you can copy files onto a recordable CD or DVD, you need additional software. There are choices here.

A packet-writing program lets you drag and drop files directly to the CD as if was a giant floppy disk. Such software is often included with new CD-RW drives, but we've often found it rather flaky. Windows XP very sensibly has packet-writing technology built in from the outset. To be fair, it's a slightly clunky implementation but it does the business dependably.

The alternative is CD recording software that lets you compile a collection of files and burn them to the disc in one hit. You can fill a disc over several sessions or 'close' (finish) the disc after just one. With CD-RW discs, you can erase files and start again; but once a CD-R disc is full, it's full forever.

Recordable DVD drives and media work in much the same way despite different underlying technology. Windows XP does not support DVD packet-writing but the next version, Longhorn, will.

Recordable compact discs are a cheap and efficient way to archive your old data.

Backup utilities

Windows 98 comes with its own backup utility called, unsurprisingly, Microsoft Backup. If it's already installed on your PC, you'll find it by clicking Start > Programs > Accessories > System Tools. If it's not there, open the Add/Remove Programs dialogue box from the Control Panel, open on the Windows Setup tab, and install Backup in the System Tools section. You'll need your original Windows 98 CD-ROM.

Backup cannot be installed so easily under Windows Millennium Edition. What you have to do is dig out your Windows Me installation CD-ROM, find the Add-ons/Msbackup folder, and double click a file called Msbexp.exe. In Windows XP

Home, you'll find it in Valueadd\MSFT\ntbackup with the file name Ntbackup.msi. Backup is installed by default in Windows XP Professional.

The beauty of Backup used to be that it supports disk spanning, which means that a backup job can be saved seamlessly across as many floppy or Zip disks as necessary. In other words, you can select as many files for backing up as you want to without worrying about their sizes: the program automatically asks for the requisite number of disks and saves the data piecemeal fashion. Restoring data is essentially just a case of running Backup in reverse and inserting the floppy disks in the right order when prompted (which adds up to one very good reason for labelling them properly as you make the original backup!)

However, with recordable CD and DVD drives now so readily available and affordable, it's much easier to perform large-scale backups. If you have too many files to fit on a single disc, just split them at some convenient point.

Microsoft Backup also supports 'incremental' backups whereby you need only copy new files or files which have changed since the last backup job. This saves you money on media and speeds up the routine. Again, though, there's little point in this when you can simply backup all your important files in a few minutes, and for a few pence. Besides, restoring files from an incremental backup is a terribly tedious business. We much prefer – and highly recommend – copying the entire contents of My Documents, plus any other key folders, with every backup. Just be sure to keep track of your file locations.

Better still, make an 'image' of your entire hard disk – that's every last file and folder – and save yourself a headache. We show you how on p68-9.

Backup is an optional extra in Windows but easily installed from the CD-ROM.

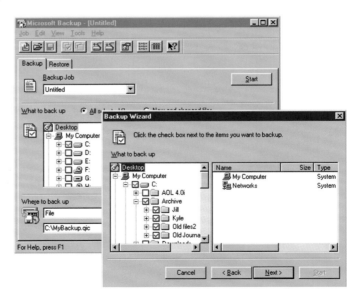

Good file management pays dividends when it comes to backing up your data.

PART **1** The tools you'll need

As we remarked earlier, fiddling with computers isn't rocket science. Nor is it brain surgery. It's a whole lot easier than replacing a car's suspension, or even the brakes on a bicycle, and it requires neither skill nor experience. Short of spilling your coffee over the motherboard, you're very unlikely to actually break your computer. However, do give yourself plenty of space to work. For even the simplest internal task, it's worthwhile shifting the whole shebang from a cramped desktop to somewhere more suitable. At the very least, ensure that you have sufficient room to work comfortably with a tower PC lying on its side.

If you can change a fuse, you can upgrade a computer.

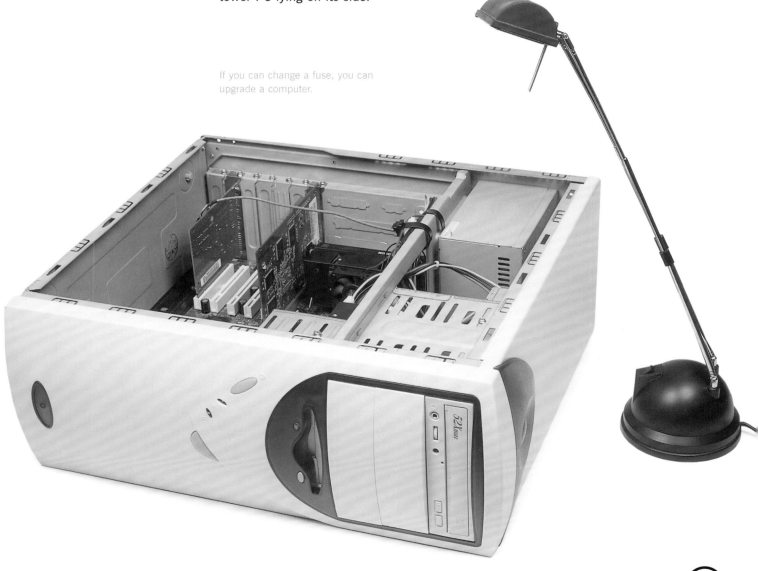

You'll need five tools to work on your PC's delicate innermost parts

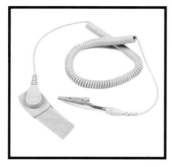

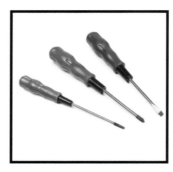

A manual for your motherboard and, ideally, all the other manuals and paperwork that came with your PC and peripherals. If your motherboard is a mystery, download a copy of Sandra (see p24) and run the Mainboard module. Now visit the manufacturer's website and cross your fingers that there's a downloadable manual available.

An antistatic wrist-strap. It won't save your life if you upgrade a running PC from the comfort of your bath but it will disperse any build-up of static electricity in your body and thus safeguard delicate circuitry from an unwelcome fry-up. Your computer will thank you for it – and so will your wallet. Wear one with pride.

Screwdrivers. One small Phillips will probably suffice – that's the one with the cross shaped pointy end – but have a flathead screwdriver to hand just in case. If you can't resist, buy one of those handy 'PC upgrade' kits.

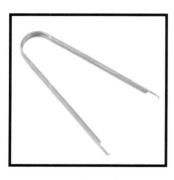

Tweezers or delicate long-nosed pliers. Essential for retrieving dropped screws.

A torch. Miniaturisation ensures a surfeit of nooks and crannies inside your computer, and they're all dark. A good adjustable desktop lamp will suffice at a pinch.

There's only one other must-have, and that's patience. Always a virtue, a measure of patience is truly essential when it comes upgrading a PC. The task at hand might not be successful at the first attempt. You might have trouble installing drivers or any of a million minor niggles may strike without warning. But don't rush it. Ever. Take your time, work through the manual that comes with any new device or component (even if it's written Jargonese, as is the norm). Think and act logically. Don't replace a hard disk on a Monday morning or network the office on a Friday afternoon when you'd rather be elsewhere.

We also strongly suggest that you back up both your important files (preferably the entire hard disk – see p68-9).

There. Now are you ready to peek inside?

PART ① Lifting the lid

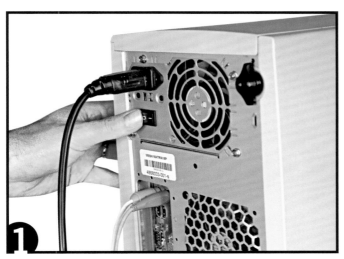

Opinions vary on *whether it's safer to leave the PC's case connected to the mains while you work – with the power turned off at the wall, of course – or to unplug it completely. Leaving it connected provides a path to earth for static electricity and protects the computer's components. It is, however, still plugged in and that just gives us the jitters. We prefer to unplug the machine and use an antistatic wrist-strap. Begin by switching off the power supply (if indeed it has an on/off switch).*

Unplug all other cables *and connectors from the back of the machine. If it helps, make a note of where everything goes, perhaps using sticky labels or diagrams. In practice, thanks to the myriad different interfaces present on the back of your PC, the plug on the end of a peripheral's cable will typically fit only one socket. The awkward connections tend to be speaker and modem cables.*

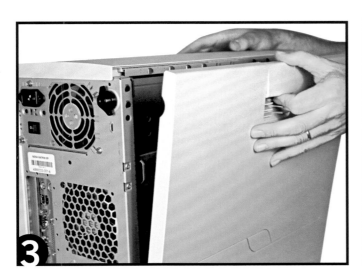

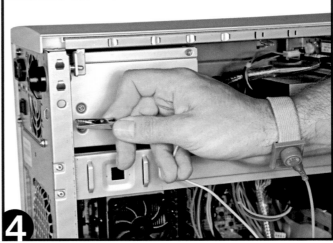

Dig out the manual *that came with your computer and figure out what holds it together. Yes, we know that sounds rather vague but there are any number of ways to screw a case together, and few of them are obvious. We've even seen designs where to get at the retaining screws you have to forcibly prise off the front of the case. Talk about counterintuitive!*

Touch something metal *like a radiator to discharge any static electricity in your body. Before going near anything internally, put on your wrist-strap and connect it to a metal part of the case. Now peer inside. Does it look like a computer? Good. Now let's make it a better one.*

PART 2

COMPUTER MANUAL

Straight to the heart

You would think, would you not, that the quickest way to speed up an ailing PC would be to give it a brainpower boost? Surprisingly, this isn't always – indeed, not even usually – the case: less radical measures are generally more effective and *much* easier.

PART

Motherboard architecture

If you understand the importance and role of the motherboard, you can do just about anything with a PC. Every area of this manual touches upon the motherboard in one way or another because this is the central component in a PC to which everything else is attached. In fact, installing a new motherboard is tantamount to building a PC from scratch rather than effecting an upgrade, and we look at this in some detail in Appendix 3.

Mouse and *keyboard* sockets.

USB Two USB interfaces for connecting external devices.

Parallel port One parallel interface, usually reserved for the printer.

Serial port Two serial interfaces for connecting external devices (hidden below parallel port).

Good reasons to replace your motherboard

You want a faster computer All motherboards support, or work with, a limited range of processors, and only those from within a given family (be this Intel's Pentium/Celeron or AMD's Athlon/Duron). The problem is that you can't simply pop a new, more powerful processor in an old motherboard and expect it to work. If you have the manual and it specifies support for a faster processor than the one you already have, then fine; but if not, a new motherboard with explicit support for the processor you want is a much safer option.

Your old motherboard has given up the ghost It's not a common failure, but it happens. If your PC is playing up, and you're sure it's down to the motherboard, the PC equivalent of open-heart surgery can save the day. Why not take the chance to upgrade to a better model at the same time?

You'd like to upgrade once and once only Many modern motherboards incorporate all the circuitry required for graphics and sound output, and often include a modem, networking and more. This makes for an economical, relatively fuss-free route to a full multimedia system.

Good reasons *not* to replace your motherboard

You may have to reformat your hard disk or at least reinstall (or, in the case of XP, reactivate) Windows. The shock of finding a whole new motherboard under the hood can induce an operating system identity crisis. Then again, a fresh software start is the perfect complement for a new motherboard.

Your old components may no longer fit Will that old ISA soundcard find a home on your swanky new motherboard? What will you do with your PCI graphics card if the new motherboard has an AGP slot? Chances are you'll have to replace your old memory modules to comply with new improved standards. If you discover that you have to buy new components throughout, it might be as cheap (and much easier) to start all over again with a new PC, perhaps hanging onto your old monitor, printer, keyboard and mouse. That said, a motherboard with integrated multimedia neatly skirts such issues.

The motherboard itself may not fit Motherboards and computer cases adhere to 'form factor' industry standards that govern size and shape so it's never safe to assume that a new motherboard will fit in an old case without first checking. By far the most popular form factor is ATX, in which a full-sized motherboard measures 305mm x 244mm and the case is designed to accommodate it. This is almost certainly what you have if your PC was made within the last seven or eight years, so finding a new ATX (or one of its smaller derivatives) shouldn't be a problem. See Appendix 3 where we install a Micro ATX motherboard in a full-sized ATX case.

Slot 1 *This is the slot design for processors, no longer in production but still in abundance.*

Memory *This is where RAM is installed. In this case, we're looking at DIMM sockets.*

CMOS battery *A replaceable battery that keeps the CMOS alive when the power is switched off. Home to all your hardware settings (see p177).*

IDE/ATA controllers *The hard disk plugs into the primary IDE/ATA channel, or controller, or socket – usually labelled IDE 1 – and the CD/DVD drive into the other.*

Floppy disk controller *Yes, the floppy disk drive plugs in here.*

AGP slot *An expansion slot reserved for a high-performance graphics card.*

BIOS *A memory chip that kick-starts a PC before Windows wakes up.*

Expansion slots *A wide variety of expansion cards can be installed in these slots to add to a PC's features. We'll look at the different types in detail on p88.*

PART 2 Upgrading RAM

Your PC's operating system requires a good deal of RAM (Random Access Memory) to run smoothly. Windows 95 needs at least 8MB to work at all, 16MB to work properly, and double that again to work smoothly. Windows 98 demands at least 16MB to get out of bed, but 64MB is a realistic minimum. Windows Millennium Edition doesn't really perform with less than 128MB, and XP ups the ante again to a whopping 256MB. Bear in mind that this is before you do anything else, anything *useful*, with your PC such as write a letter or send an email. Every program you fire up operates in RAM, and every document, picture or file resides there too for as long as it's 'open'.

DDR RAM.

SD RAM.

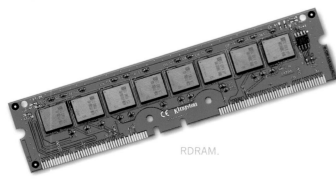

RDRAM.

When the available memory begins to run out, as it invariably does, the first thing you notice is a general slow down in operations. Come the point of RAM overload, the PC has four choices: give up and crash; freeze unhelpfully; refuse to do another thing until you close down some programs; or magic some more RAM out of thin air. Thankfully, the last option is first to be followed. Windows reserves an area of the hard disk for use as a kind of pretend, or virtual, memory (and calls it a swap file). This keeps things ticking over but it's woefully inefficient compared to using real RAM. If you hear your hard disk whirring and clicking a lot as you work, this is a sign of 'thrashing' – the disk struggling to keep up with the pressure as Windows constantly swaps data between it and RAM. Despite the name, it's not painful but it does nothing for performance. All of which leads us to one inescapable conclusion: RAM is good and more is better. What's more, it's also very straightforward to install extra memory.

What you need to know

Inevitably, RAM comes in assorted flavours and you have to be sure to buy the right type for your particular PC. Here's a guide to the critical specifications.

Capacity RAM modules are measured in megabytes and are available in several sizes, including 32, 64, 128, 256 and 512MB. We looked at how to establish how much RAM you already have onboard back on p22-24.

All motherboards support up to but not beyond a given quota of RAM, but the figures vary. A brand new motherboard might support 4GB, which is much more than you'd ever need, whereas an older model might peg out at 768MB or less. If you need a lot of memory for, say, editing digital video or working with high resolution digital images, you may find that a new motherboard with increased RAM support is a sensible purchase.

Type Like everything else in the PC world, RAM has evolved apace. Brand new systems might come with souped-up versions called RD RAM or DDR RAM (Rambus Dynamic and Double Data Rate

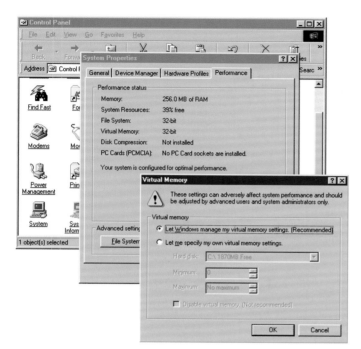

Windows uses the hard disk to make up for any RAM deficiency. A proper memory upgrade is much more efficient.

RAM modules sit in slots on the motherboard.

memory, respectively), but your existing system will probably have SD (Synchronous Dynamic) RAM installed. It's time to check your motherboard manual, or dig out the order/delivery paperwork just to make sure.

Connector RAM comes in modules loaded with storage cells that sit in slots on the motherboard. There are three main types – SIMM (Single Inline Memory Module); DIMM (Dual Inline Memory Module); and RIMM (Rambus Inline Memory Module) – and you simply can't mix and match. To install extra RAM, you either use a free slot on the motherboard or, if necessary, replace an existing RAM module with a higher capacity version e.g. ditch a measly 16MB module to free up space for a 256MB module.

One complication, and an important one, is that SIMMs must be grouped together in pairs, or 'banks', where each module has the same capacity. The motherboard in a typical older Pentium PC would have four sockets (i.e. two banks), so possible configurations would include:

1st bank	2 x 16MB SIMMs
2nd bank	2 x 16MB SIMMs
Total RAM	64MB

1st bank	2 x 16MB SIMMs
2nd bank	2 x 32MB SIMMs
Total RAM	96MB

What you *can't* do is pluck one 16MB SIMM from its home and replace it with a 32MB module unless you simultaneously do the same with its partner. DIMMs have no such restriction. We might also add that if your motherboard has SIMM-style slots, you really should be thinking about scrapping it in favour of a DIMM model. Curiously, Rambus memory complicates matters again. RIMM modules must be installed in matching pairs, just like the old SIMMs, and you have to fill any unused sockets with dummy modules called Continuity RIMMs.

Speed It may seem odd to think of memory in terms of speed, but RAM modules talk to the processor at different rates. This is important because it relates to the speed of the chipset on the motherboard, so again check the motherboard manual and be sure to buy memory modules that the motherboard supports.

Buying RAM

By far the easiest way to establish a motherboard/memory match is with a web-based configuration utility. Just enter the make and model of your motherboard and you'll be shown a list of compatible modules. See:

www.kingston.com/ukroot

and

www.crucial.com/uk/index.asp

But how exactly can you glean the required motherboard information? Well, the easiest way is by checking the motherboard manual or the paperwork that shipped with your computer. Alternatively, don't be shy about calling your computer supplier and asking what they put under the hood. They should be able to give you the motherboard model by checking your order or simply by reference to the system name. Failing that, you may be lucky enough to find an obvious manufacturer's stamp on the motherboard itself.

Another alternative is the Belarc Advisor (**www.belarc.com/free_download.html**). This is a free downloadable utility that summarises system information in a handy and relatively clear format. In this screenshot, for instance, we can see that the PC has a total of 1,024MB of RAM installed as two 512MB modules. The motherboard – or Main Circuit Board – is a Gigabyte 8PE667P. Armed with this information, we could turn to the Kingston or Crucial memory configuration utilities

Use the Belarc Advisor to reveal your motherboard's secrets

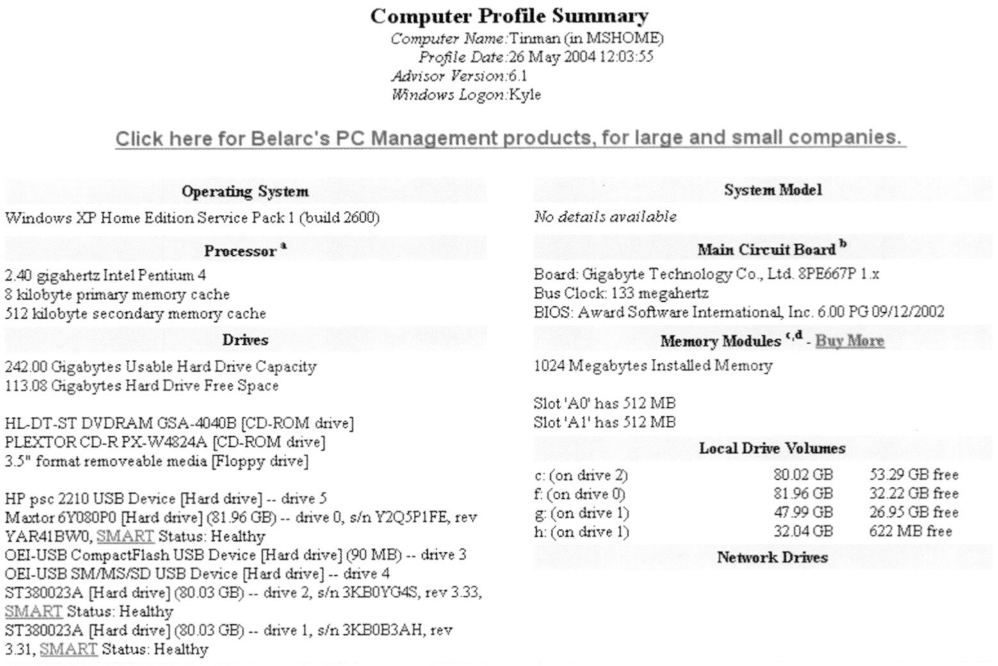

Computer Profile Summary

Computer Name: Tinman (in MSHOME)
Profile Date: 26 May 2004 12:03:55
Advisor Version: 6.1
Windows Logon: Kyle

<u>Click here for Belarc's PC Management products, for large and small companies.</u>

Operating System

Windows XP Home Edition Service Pack 1 (build 2600)

Processor [a]

2.40 gigahertz Intel Pentium 4
8 kilobyte primary memory cache
512 kilobyte secondary memory cache

Drives

242.00 Gigabytes Usable Hard Drive Capacity
113.08 Gigabytes Hard Drive Free Space

HL-DT-ST DVDRAM GSA-4040B [CD-ROM drive]
PLEXTOR CD-R PX-W4824A [CD-ROM drive]
3.5" format removeable media [Floppy drive]

HP psc 2210 USB Device [Hard drive] -- drive 5
Maxtor 6Y080P0 [Hard drive] (81.96 GB) -- drive 0, s/n Y2Q5P1FE, rev YAR41BW0, <u>SMART</u> Status: Healthy
OEI-USB CompactFlash USB Device [Hard drive] (90 MB) -- drive 3
OEI-USB SM/MS/SD USB Device [Hard drive] -- drive 4
ST380023A [Hard drive] (80.03 GB) -- drive 2, s/n 3KB0YG4S, rev 3.33, <u>SMART</u> Status: Healthy
ST380023A [Hard drive] (80.03 GB) -- drive 1, s/n 3KB0B3AH, rev 3.31, <u>SMART</u> Status: Healthy

System Model

No details available

Main Circuit Board [b]

Board: Gigabyte Technology Co., Ltd. 8PE667P 1.x
Bus Clock: 133 megahertz
BIOS: Award Software International, Inc. 6.00 PG 09/12/2002

Memory Modules [c,d] - <u>Buy More</u>

1024 Megabytes Installed Memory

Slot 'A0' has 512 MB
Slot 'A1' has 512 MB

Local Drive Volumes

c: (on drive 2)	80.02 GB	53.29 GB free
f: (on drive 0)	81.96 GB	32.22 GB free
g: (on drive 1)	47.99 GB	26.95 GB free
h: (on drive 1)	32.04 GB	622 MB free

Network Drives

These 184-pin DIMM modules are compatible with your system.

1GB — CT12864Z265	DDR PC2100	CL=2.5	Non-parity		US $249.99 (each)	Buy
1GB — CT12864Z335	DDR PC2700	CL=2.5	Non-parity		US $271.99 (each)	Buy
1GB — CT12864Z40B	DDR PC3200	CL=3	Non-parity		US $389.99 (each)	Buy
512MB — CT6464Z335	DDR PC2700	CL=2.5	Non-parity		US $99.99 (each)	Buy
Most Popular! 512MB — CT6464Z265	DDR PC2100	CL=2.5	Non-parity		US $100.99 (each)	Buy
512MB — CT6464Z40B	DDR PC3200	CL=3	Non-parity		US $105.99 (each)	Buy
256MB — CT3264Z265	DDR PC2100	CL=2.5	Non-parity		US $55.99 (each)	Buy
256MB — CT3264Z40B	DDR PC3200	CL=3	Non-parity		US $57.99 (each)	Buy
256MB — CT3264Z335	DDR PC2700	CL=2.5	Non-parity		US $57.99 (each)	Buy
128MB — CT1664Z265	DDR PC2100	CL=2.5	Non-parity		US $31.99 (each)	Buy
128MB — CT1664Z335	DDR PC2700	CL=2.5	Non-parity		US $31.99 (each)	Buy
128MB — CT1664Z40B	DDR PC3200	CL=3	Non-parity		US $31.99 (each)	Buy

The Crucial online memory configuration utility makes choosing memory simple.

mentioned above and uncover our upgrade options (not that a PC with 1GB of RAM really needs an upgrade, you understand, but the principle holds true regardless).

This we did, and found out that:

- The motherboard has three 184-pin DIMM slots (two of which we know from the Belarc Advisor are already filled)
- It supports a maximum of 2,048MB RAM (so our best upgrade option would presumably be a 1,024MB module – but read on)
- It supports two different speeds of memory (PC2100 and PC2700, to be precise). We could conceivably use an even faster flavour of RAM like PC3200 but we wouldn't see any real-world benefit.

Having come this far, the next step is paying the motherboard manufacturer's website a visit and looking for further details on this particular motherboard. This is important mainly to establish whether there are any restrictions governing module support. If you check the Support section of the website, you might be lucky and find a downloadable manual for your particular motherboard.

We did – and a good job it was, too. Buying a 1GB (1,024MB) module for the vacant DIMM slot on this Gigabyte motherboard would have been a costly mistake. The trouble here is that the motherboard supports only four banks of memory, which equates to two double-sided modules or one double-sided module plus one or two single-sided modules. It already has two double-sided modules *in situ* so further upgrades are out of the question. In fact, the only possibility is replacing one of the existing modules with another of a higher capacity.

But the details in this example don't really matter. What does matter is the point that you have to check carefully before making a purchase.

GIGABYTE
TECHNOLOGY

繁體中文 | Contact Us | Site Map

Home | Company | Products | Support | Awards | News | Where to Buy

Worldwide
Select Languages

Home > Products > Motherboard > Products > **GA-8PE667 Pro**

Find   What are you looking for?

> Enlarge View

Overview
Awards
BIOS
Certification
Comparison Sheet
CPU support list
Driver
FAQ
Manual
News

GA-8PE667 Pro
Intel 845PE chipset
Processor
1. Socket 478 for Intel® Pentium® 4 with HT Technology
Chipset
1. Intel® 82845PE MCH
2. Intel® 82801DB ICH4
3. Intel® PRO/100 VE LAN chip
4. Realtek ALC650E Audio AC'97 CODEC
5. Super I/O: ITE I/O IT8712F chip
6. 2 x 3M bit flash ROM
Front Side Bus
1. 533/400 MHz FSB
Memory
1. Type: DDR266/333 (PC2100/2700) 184 pin (2.5v)
2. 3 x DIMM
3. Max capacity: Up to 2 GB

Here we tracked down our motherboard model to the manufacturer's website. The Manual link on the left leads to a downloadable copy of the long-lost paper manual originally supplied with the system.

Step 2: Install memory modules

The motherboard has 3 dual inline memory module (DIMM) sockets, but it can only support a maximum of 4 banks of DDR memory. DDR sockets 1 uses 2 banks, DDR sockets 2&3 share the remaining 2 banks. Please refer to the following tables for possible memory configurations supported. The BIOS will automatically detects memory type and size. To install the memory module, just push it vertically into the DIMM socket. The DIMM module can only fit in one direction due to the notch. Memory size can vary between sockets.

Support Unbuffered DDR DIMM Sizes type:

64 Mbit (2Mx8x4 banks)	64 Mbit (1Mx16x4 banks)	128 Mbit(4Mx8x4 banks)
128 Mbit(2Mx16x4 banks)	256 Mbit(8Mx8x4 banks)	256 Mbit(4Mx16x4 banks)
512 Mbit(16Mx8x4 banks)	512 Mbit(8Mx16x4 banks)	
Total System Memory (Max2GB)		

Notes: Double-sided x16 DDR memory devices are not support by Intel 845E/G /PE/GE chipset.

Install memory in any combination table:

DDR1	DDR2	DDR3
S	S	S
D	S	
D	D	X
D	X	D
S	D	X
S	X	D

D:Double Sided DIMM S:Single Sided DIMM

DDR

Oops. Our motherboard already has a full complement of double-sided memory modules and cannot be further upgraded without sacrificing one of the existing 512MB modules. Better to learn this now than later.

PART

Step-by-step RAM upgrade

Installing a new RAM module is easy. Here we add a second module alongside an existing one. With DIMMs, you would normally install a second module in the slot labelled DIMM 2 and a third in DIMM 3 but be sure to follow the motherboard manual's directions and restrictions.

Before attempting *any internal work on your PC, re-read the safety precautions on p33.*

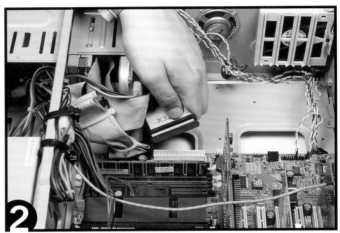

Ensure that *you have clear access to the RAM slots. This might mean temporarily removing other components or unplugging cables. Just be sure to put everything back the way you find it. Making notes is a good idea.*

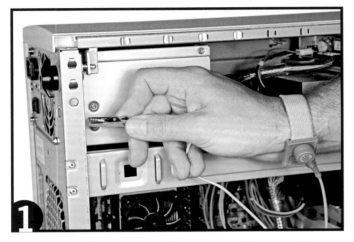

The DIMM socket *has a locking tab at either end. Press down on these tabs to open them.*

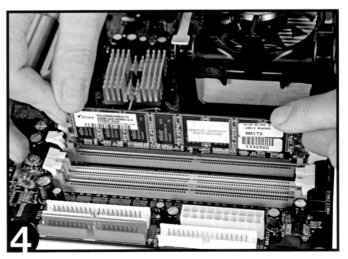

Carefully remove *your new module from its antistatic bag and, holding it gently by the edges, align the notches on the lower edge of the module with those in the slot.*

5

Press down firmly on the module until it sits level in the slot. Be sure to keep it vertical. As you push it home, the locking tabs should engage with the keyed ends of the module and snap shut. Give them a helping hand, or finger, if necessary.

6

When both tabs have locked into place, the module will be held securely in the slot and you can consider the installation complete. Now replace anything that you set asunder earlier in order to access the sockets.

```
AMIBIOS(C)2001 American Megatrends, Inc.
BIOS Date: 02/19/03 19:39:18  Ver: 08.00.02

Press DEL to run Setup
Checking NVRAM..

196MB OK

Auto-Detecting Pri Master..IDE Hard Disk
Auto-Detecting Pri Slave...Not Detected
Auto-Detecting Sec Master..CDROM
Auto-Detecting Sec Slave...
```

7

When you restart the computer, watch the screen carefully. When the system runs through its standard start-up procedure, check that the total RAM reported is now what you would expect e.g. if you just installed a 128MB into a system with 64MB, the total should now be 196MB. And that's it: no fuss with drivers, no fiddly configuration, just a much improved PC. Enjoy.

 TROUBLE-SHOOTER

If the RAM upgrade does not register when you start the system, check the details in the General tab of Device Manager (see p23-24). If this looks right, reboot and try again.

Still not registering? Repeat the installation process and ensure that the new module is properly locked in place. Also try running a Belarc Advisor report.

If this is a SIMM upgrade, check that you've followed the bank rules, i.e. installed two SIMMs of equal capacity in each bank.

As a final test, remove the new module and move one of the existing modules (DIMM only) into the now-vacant socket. Restart and ensure that the original

quantity of RAM still registers. This way, you'll confirm that you're doing everything correctly; the socket itself is fine; and the new module must be faulty. Exchange it!

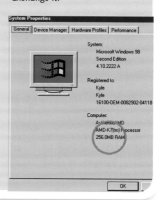

PART

Understanding processors

Imagine this manual was double its current size. Now double it again. Now cram it full of hieroglyphic tables, small print, warnings, disclaimers and impenetrable jargon. You *still* wouldn't have enough information on hand to perform a processor upgrade in all possible circumstances. There are just too many angles, too many possibilities, too many permutations to cover all bases. This book is much too short to make such an attempt. So is life.

But surely, you protest, it's merely a matter of out with the old and in with the new? How hard can it be? Well, the physical procedure for changing the component is indeed straightforward, but getting to that point is fraught with difficulties. The first really seriously limiting factor is whether a new processor will even fit onto your existing motherboard.

The most common connectors

A processor installs in the motherboard either in a slot, much like a memory module, or flat in a socket. Slot designs have been ditched by both Intel and AMD, the two leading manufacturers of processors, in favour of sockets.

Socket 7 A flat socket on the motherboard. Compatible processors include Pentium and Pentium MMX; AMD K6; Cyrix 6x86 MX and MII.

Slot 1 A groove in which the processor cartridge sits on edge. Compatible processors include Intel Celeron, Pentium II and Pentium III.

Socket 370 A newer style socket. Compatible processors include Intel Celeron and Pentium III (yes, these two ranges are available in both slot and socket designs).

Slot A Similar to Slot 1 but designed exclusively for AMD's Athlon and Duron ranges.

Socket A (also known as Socket 462) An alternative socket approach for AMD Athlon and Duron processors.

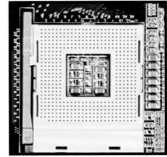

Slot A The most popular of the lot these past few years. Socket 478 plays host to Intel Pentium 4 and Celeron processors.

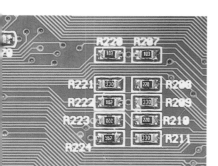

A motherboard bus.

Keeping cool is a critical consideration for processors, hence the need for bulky heatsinks.

What you need to know (and worry about)

The slot/socket compatibility issue is only one consideration. Others include:

System bus speed (also known as the front side bus). The rate at which data is handled by the motherboard, which determines the true speed of a PC. A processor can work flat out for all its worth but if the motherboard (or, more precisely, the chipset) can't process its results quickly enough, that equates to a lot of wasted effort. Most motherboards include a feature called a multiplier that enables them to accept faster processors than they were originally designed for, but there are constraints – see Techie Corner opposite.

Cooling All processors must be adequately cooled and the faster they run, the hotter they get. The standard cooling mechanism for a socket-based processor is a solid-state contraption called a heatsink that sits on top of the processor and dissipates heat through convection and with the help of a built-in fan. When buying a new processor, always insist on a 'boxed' or 'retail' (as opposed to an OEM, original equipment manufacturer) version. As the name suggests, it comes in a branded box but is also supplied with a compatible heatsink/fan unit. You can buy these units separately but you'd be ill-advised to do so unless you are absolutely confident that it offers sufficient cooling for your particular processor.

The BIOS chip If your computer was manufactured before the processor to which you now want to upgrade was developed, as is likely, the motherboard may not recognise or work with the new chip. Motherboards are usually designed with some built-in forward compatibility but only ever within certain limits. A subsequent significant change in processor architecture could make an easy upgrade impossible, even though a new processor physically fits the old socket.

One possible solution is a BIOS upgrade, which involves downloading a program from the motherboard manufacturer's website and 'flashing' the BIOS chip with a set of updated instructions. However, BIOS upgrades are not always available. Even when they are, they can't always ready an older motherboard for a newer processor. So, unless your motherboard already offers explicit support for the processor you wish to install, as confirmed by the manual or manufacturer's website, we'd strongly suggest going for a new motherboard at the same time as upgrading the processor. See Appendix 3 for details.

Voltages Does your motherboard support the required voltage of the processor? As a rule, modern processors run at lower voltages (i.e. cooler) than their predecessors, and a 3.3v model will soon blow up or burn out in a 5v socket. It's vital to check that your motherboard and processor upgrade are compatible. Again, may we suggest that a new motherboard makes sense?

Speed demon For all their power, processors deal exclusively in the 1s and 0s of binary code. That in itself sounds baffling until you consider that a 1 is merely a signal generated by an electric current ('on') and a 0 the lack of such a signal ('off'). The code 101, for instance, translates as power on–off–on again. The

TECHIE CORNER

The good news is that most post-Pentium processors are perfectly fast enough to cope with most computer work, short of running intensive multimedia applications and playing the latest games. If it's graphical performance you need, consider installing a new graphics card instead (p90). The benefits will be far greater than those to be had by swapping the processor alone. Likewise, a PC's overall performance can be better improved by increasing the amount of RAM on tap (p42), because this gives it more working space.

Remember all that 'Apollo missions were run on a calculator' stuff from the opening pages? It's time for a reality check. Do you really need a processor running at two billion clock cycles per second? No, you don't. Or if your computer usage is so intensive and demanding that you really do need a super-super-superfast processor at the helm, then you also need a brand new state-of-the- art system crammed with the latest complementary devices to support it. In other words, forget about an upgrade and buy a new system instead – or simply upgrade the motherboard, as described in Appendix 3.

BIOS (Basic Input/Output System) is a chip on the motherboard that controls the fundamental operations of a computer.

So-called boxed processors are supplied with compatible heatsinks. This is the only safe way to buy one.

processor then runs these signals through its many, many microscopic transistors, interprets them according to certain logical rules, and outputs a binary response. Simple, huh? It's all controlled by an internal clock (of sorts) that beats at a certain rate. A 1GHz processor ticks one billion (yes, *billion*) times every single second, with each tick representing an opportunity for the processor to do something useful. Thus a 1GHz processor can do more work in a shorter time than a 500MHz (500 million ticks per second) model.

But it's not *all* about speed. A fast processor in an old system will run like a Ferrari in a car park, and you will virtually always see a much greater gain by slotting in an extra slice of RAM.

Here's a quick glance at how quickly Intel processors have evolved:

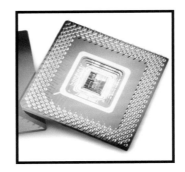

Pentium – *1993*
60–200MHz

Pentium Pro – *1995*
150–200MHz

Pentium MMX – *1997*
166–233MHz

Pentium II – *1997*
233–450MHz

Pentium III – *1999*
450–1.13GHz

Pentium 4 – *2000*
1.3–3.4 GHz . . . and rising

TECHIE CORNER

ZIF ZIF stands for Zero Insertion Force and describes the mechanism used to install processors in motherboard sockets. Rather than you having to forcibly pry a processor out of its socket with clumsy fingers or a screwdriver, a little lever unlocks the socket so you can lift the chip out cleanly. Older PCs often have a LIF socket (the L stands for Low), in which case there's no lever and you need a special tool called a (wait for it) chip remover to gently prise the processor free. But be careful when putting a processor into a LIF socket – the force required is not at all that low and perilously close to that required to crack the motherboard. Intel recommends against home replacements of LIF chips. This is sound advice that we happily endorse.

Intel or AMD? Quite frankly, who cares? The only thing duller than a debate about the relative merits of the Intel P4 versus the AMD Athlon is the equally interminable competition between devotees of the PC and the Apple Mac. Both camps thoroughly befuddle the consumer with incomprehensible numbering systems – Intel's currently rewriting the rules all over again – and making like-for-like comparisons is as tricky as it is fruitless. The truth is that a recent processor from either manufacturer will do you very nicely indeed, and you can certainly save a packet by opting for a version that's a few months old rather than the absolute latest model.

There's not much to choose between Intel and AMD processors on the page and precious little when they're installed in your PC.

Installing a new processor

When you buy a boxed or retail processor, full instructions are provided. There's really nothing to it. Here we look at the process for a Pentium 4. It's virtually identical for an AMD Athlon, although the processor socket and heatsink designs are slightly different.

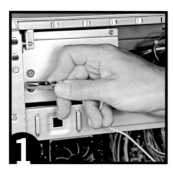

Before attempting any internal work on your PC, re-read the safety precautions on p33.

The existing heatsink is connected by a thin cable to a three-pin power socket on the motherboard. Locate this and unplug the cable. Now free the heatsink from its tether to the motherboard – it should have a fairly obvious release mechanism – and remove from the case.

Raise the ZIF lever that runs along the side of the socket and carefully remove the old processor. Examine the socket and you will see that the corner adjacent to the lever's hinge is missing two pin-holes. This is known as the Pin 1 position.

Holding the new processor by the edges only, check the pin array on its underside. One corner will also be missing two pins and marked with a gold triangle. This is Pin 1 position on the processor.

The trick is now to position the processor in the motherboard socket matching Pin 1 to Pin 1. No pressure should be required to complete this operation: simply drop the processor into place. When you are confident that the processor is seated securely in its socket with no gaps around the edges, lower the lever to lock it into place.

There has to be a thermal bond between the base of the heatsink and the top of the processor. This will be supplied as a glue-like substance in a syringe or tube, or as a self-adhesive pad, or, as here, pre-applied to the heatsink base.

Now install the heatsink according to the directions supplied. It will attach securely to a frame surrounding the socket (in the case of an Intel Pentium) or to the socket itself (in the case of an AMD Athlon). Finally, connect the heatsink power cable to the same motherboard power socket as the old heatsink. Job done.

3

PART 3 Adding a new drive

Breathing new life into an ailing PC with major surgery is one thing, but there's more than one way to skin a cat (or mix a metaphor). Some of these upgrades will boost its performance, others will prolong its useful lifespan, but all will make your PC a more productive tool and/or a better toy.

PART 3 Why upgrade your hard disk?

Here's a funny thing: no matter why you first bought your PC, you're almost certainly using it for something entirely different now. As we become more proficient and confident, we explore new avenues and discover just what all this hardware and software can really do for us. Thus it's no surprise to find a book-keeping machine roped into editing digital video or a system purchased primarily for internet access functioning as a full-blown home entertainment centre. That's why upgrading a PC is so often a compelling, and frequently pressing, affair.

One of the key components that comes under pressure soonest is the hard disk. It's amazing just how quickly a seemingly cavernous disk can fill to capacity. A single megabyte might be sufficient storage space for the entire text of a novel, but that equates to a mere six seconds or so of uncompressed music. Throw in a few high resolution images or video files and take into account the size of modern software applications, including the operating system itself, and it's little wonder that we run out of space sooner than we thought possible. This is when our thoughts turn to upgrading the hard disk.

When your hard disk falls behind the times, it's time to upgrade.

Short of disk space? This external model provides a staggering terabyte (1,024GB) of extra capacity.

Zip drives can back up 100, 250 or 750MB of data per disk. They are, however, increasingly uncommon and not a great investment for the future.

How to upgrade...

There are essentially three upgrade options. First, you may install a secondary hard disk alongside your existing one. This is akin to building a warehouse in the car park, providing additional space without changing your current working environment. Alternatively, you may prefer to *replace* your existing hard disk. This has the virtue of neatness but the distinct disadvantages that you must also reinstall the operating system from scratch and somehow transfer all your existing files onto the new disk. Of course, if your original disk was to suddenly fail – a rare occurrence but always a possibility – this might be your only option (at which point, needless to say, the value of having a good, recent backup or, preferably, a disk image becomes all too apparent).

Finally, you may plump for an external hard disk. We look at the ups and downs of this approach in a moment.

...and how not to

If storage space is your only concern, do consider removable media before splashing out on a new disk. For instance, a recordable CD or DVD drive could help you permanently archive all your older files and thus lighten the load on the hard disk. A single DVD holds 4.7GB so it's easy to salvage considerable space.

A simple zip software utility can also shrink your files without removing them from the disk and Windows has a few other tools that can clear out clutter. See Part 7 for details.

You might also consider a Zip or Jaz drive. We, however, would not. Even after all these years of mass production, both the drives and the media – that is, blank disks and cartridges – remain surprisingly expensive. There is also the problem of compatibility: if you archive files onto Zip disks, you can only copy them to or access them from another computer if it too has a Zip drive installed. By contrast, you can read and copy files on a home-burned CD or DVD with virtually every PC on the planet.

Iomega's Jaz drive holds 2GB per cartridge. A blank recordable DVD has more than double the capacity and costs a fraction of the price.

What you need to know

The hard disk is a device used for storing data. Unlike RAM, where data is held in a kind of dynamic flux, files once saved to the hard disk are housed in safe storage. These files can, of course, be retrieved from the hard disk and altered, deleted or simply re-saved at will, but they don't disappear when the power is switched off. The hard disk drive is the mechanism that controls the disk, including the magnetic heads that do the hard work and the case in which it's all held. But since the disk and the drive are in practice inseparable, we'll just talk about disks.

So how do you go about choosing a new one?

Capacity Without question, size matters when it comes to hard disks. Modern disks top 200GB and we'd certainly suggest that 60–80GB is the absolute minimum for a secondary disk.

Speed #1 Not an obvious consideration, perhaps, but hard disks spin at different rates. You'll see rotational (or spindle) speeds of 5,400rpm, 7,200rpm and 10,000rpm, and it doesn't hurt to get the nimblest disk that you can afford. The faster the disk spins, the faster it can spit out data to your eagerly waiting computer. Note, however, that it's never worth upgrading a hard disk for speed alone. We're talking about differences on the scale of milliseconds.

Speed #2 The speed that matters more involves something called direct memory access (DMA), a process whereby data moves from the hard disk into RAM without going through the processor. Look for ratings of 33, 66, 100 and even 133 megabytes per second. This is the measure of the drive's theoretical maximum data throughput. But even if the faster option is within budget, check the rating of the IDE/ATA interface on your motherboard. Installing a 100MB/sec disk on a 66MB/sec motherboard is a waste of time.

Mounting brackets enable a 3.5 inch drive to use a 5.25 inch bay.

Speed #3 Just to throw a spanner in the works, the truth is that DMA data throughput itself is rather misleading. What really matters is the sustained data transfer rate i.e. the speed at which the drive transfers data over a prolonged period of average activity, not just in frantic bursts. Naturally, you'll find this information hard to come by. Rather than relying upon the manufacturer's data, look for independent tests and reviews in computer magazines and websites. Or just accept that any hard disk with a spindle speed of 7,200rpm and rated for a 66MB/sec interface (known as EIDE Ultra66 or ATA/66) is probably more than sufficient for your every need.

Drive size Internal hard disks are 3.5-inch drives. This is fine so long as you have a free 3.5-inch drive bay available – and you'll probably have to open up the case to find out – but otherwise you'll need a special mounting bracket to secure it in a 5.25-inch bay. Such a bracket may or may not come in the box, so check first.

Check the specification carefully before buying a new hard disk.

Selecting cables… and cable select

As we discuss in a moment, a standard hard disk connects to the motherboard by means of a flat ribbon IDE/ATA cable. Four important points here:

● Ribbon cables are not all the same, although you could be forgiven for thinking so. Certainly, any cable will fit any drive and motherboard. However, older cables have only 40 internal wires, or conductors, whereas newer cables have 80. For all new drives, an 80-wire cable is a must. The extra wires reduce signal interference.

● If you want to install a second hard disk alongside your existing disk, you'll need a cable with three connectors: one for the motherboard and one each for the drives. You may well find a suitable cable in the box when you buy a new drive but this isn't guaranteed.

● Note that the IDE/ATA ribbon cable is coloured pink or red along one edge. This corresponds to 'Pin 1' and is there to ensure that you connect the cable correctly. Always identify the Pin 1 position on both your drive and the motherboard socket before making a cable connection. It should be clearly marked but you may have to consult the manual.

● Where two drives share a socket (or channel, to be precise), one must be designated the 'master' and one the 'slave'. This merely indicates the order in which Windows allocates drive letters to devices (for instance, C: to the master drive and D: to the slave). There are two ways to determine master/slave status. Hard drives have 'jumpers', or little plastic sheaths that sit over an array of pins in a number of possible patterns. The pin arrangement tells the motherboard that a particular drive is the master or the slave on the channel. The trouble starts if you mistakenly configure both drives as the master or slave, in which case neither will work.

There is an easier way, however, and that's setting the jumpers to a third possible position called Cable Select. As the name suggests, the cable itself then decides which drive is which. It's a simple business: the drive connected to the far end of the cable – i.e. the opposite end to the motherboard – is automatically the master.

To install a second hard disk, you'll need a cable with three connectors.

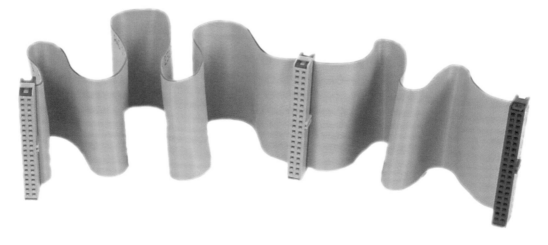

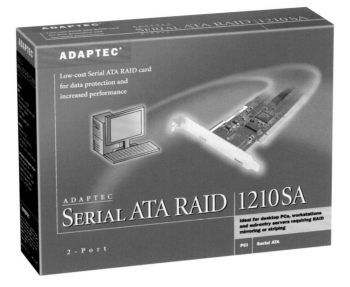

RAID

RAID stands for Redundant Array of Independent Disks, which doesn't sound too promising. However, this is a method – or rather several methods – of combining multiple hard disks to best advantage.

At its simplest, when you install a new hard disk, be it internal or external, you gain some extra storage space. That's probably precisely what you wanted and you'll be happy to leave it at that. The new drive will show up in Windows with its own drive letter and you copy files to and from it with ease using Windows Explorer or any other file management program. You can also save files directly to the drive.

With RAID, though, you can go further. The two main techniques are called 'striping' and 'mirroring'. With striping, also called RAID level 0, you can treat two drives exactly as if they were a single device. For instance, if you have a 30GB hard disk and install a new 160GB upgrade, you can 'stripe' them to appear to Windows as a single 190GB drive. The sole advantage of this is faster performance, because data can be saved to and read from the separate disks simultaneously. This improves the overall sustained transfer rate (see Speed #3 on p53). The trouble is that if one disk fails, recovering data from the other may prove impossible. In other words, striping is high performance but high risk.

With mirroring, or RAID Level 1, all data saved to one drive is simultaneously copied to the second drive. This is thus a kind of instantaneous backup regime: if the primary disk should fail, you're guaranteed to have a copy of all lost files. On the other hand, the new drive won't offer any additional storage capacity.

It's possible to combine striping and mirroring for performance plus security, but this requires four drives. There are also several other RAID possibilities – Levels 2 through to 6 – that offer degrees of error correction and fault tolerance.

If any of this appeals, you'll need to buy a RAID adapter. This is an expansion card that provides additional hard disk interfaces (IDE/ATA or preferably SATA) and the hardware/software to run RAID successfully. Alternatively, many new motherboards come with RAID capability built in. Be sure to look for this at the time of purchase.

A word of warning

If your motherboard is of a certain age, there may be three distinct problems with its BIOS. On one hand, it may not recognise disks larger than 504MB, in which case your new device is going to be invisible to the PC. On another hand, if the BIOS is a little younger but still no spring chicken, it may not recognise disks larger than 8GB – in which case ditto. However, many drives come with slick software that can circumvent these issues, and you could always upgrade the BIOS first. Note that if your motherboard has EIDE controllers onboard (as opposed to plain IDE), no problem: your BIOS is just fine.

But on the third and final hand, only a 'plug and play' BIOS chip will automatically recognise a new hard disk and supply CMOS (see Appendix 1) with all the information it needs (specifically, how many cylinders, heads and sectors the disk has). Failing that, you'll have to manually enter all this stuff in CMOS yourself. Although this isn't actually too difficult, it can seem a daunting, non-intuitive procedure for a novice and we wouldn't recommend it unless you're absolutely confident of getting it right. Our advice would be to consider an internal hard disk upgrade only if you are sure your BIOS supports large drives and recognises them automatically. Once again, dig out the manual or visit the manufacturer's website.

Interface face-off

When it comes to installing a new hard disk or, indeed, any other kind of drive, the first consideration is how to connect it to the rest of the computer system. What it needs is an interface of some description i.e. a gateway that enables the exchange of data between the drive and the rest of the PC through the motherboard; or a socket into which it can plug. There are, of course, several possibilities.

IDE adaptors should be clearly marked on the motherboard. If not, they're easy enough to find.

IDE/ATA (Integrated Drive Electronics/Advanced Technology Attachment) The most common interface for hard disk and CD drives, IDE/ATA hides under various nicknames (see Techie Corner opposite). Virtually all motherboards have one or two IDE/ATA interfaces (or host adapters) onboard, depending upon their age. In most cases, the hard disk is connected to one controller and the CD-ROM drive to the other, both by means of flat, wide ribbon-like cables. If you examine each ribbon, you may or may not find a spare connector somewhere along its length. This is because each IDE/ATA interface is a channel that can host two separate drives. This allows a total of four drives to be connected to the motherboard. If the ribbon in your PC does not have a spare connector, you'll need to replace it before installing an extra drive (see the Selecting cables section on p54).

The advantages of going down the IDE/ATA route are pretty compelling: your PC already has the requisite sockets in place, and the vast majority of drives come ready equipped to plug in and play with a minimum of fuss. However...

If you already have four drives in your system – two hard disks, a CD and a DVD drive, say – you can add extra IDE/ATA interfaces with an expansion card.

SCSI (Small Computer System Interface, but just call it 'scuzzy') SCSI is an alternative channel with one big benefit over IDE/ATA, namely that multiple devices can share a single adaptor. So, instead of a maximum of four devices sharing two IDE/ATA channels, a SCSI-equipped PC can have 7 or 15 devices all daisy-chained together – or even more if it has a second SCSI adaptor. What's more, SCSI drives can be considerably faster than their IDE/ATA counterparts.

But there are disadvantages. One is simply the cost: gigabyte for gigabyte, SCSI devices are more expensive to buy. The other is that motherboards do not generally come with a SCSI adaptor onboard, which means that you have to fit one yourself before installing a SCSI device. This is as simple as fitting an expansion card, of which much more shortly, but it does use up a

A SCSI adaptor expansion card adds a new dimension to your drive possibilities but it's far from essential in a domestic computer.

This PCI expansion card has no less than four internal Serial ATA sockets.

From left to right we see: an older 40-wire IDE/ATA cable, an 80-wire version – essential for fast hard disks – and the new skinny Serial ATA cable.

free expansion slot and adds considerably to the cost (and hassle). Besides which, the difference in speed between a SCSI drive and an IDE/ATA drive is negligible in normal use, and it's really only servers that benefit from multiple device support. SCSI makes little practical sense for the average desktop system.

Serial ATA If you buy a new motherboard today, there's a good chance that it will have an alternative hard disk interface either alongside or as a replacement for traditional IDE/ATA channels. Enter Serial ATA, or SATA. This is, we are assured, the interface of the future, offering data throughput of 150MB per second. This betters the current and final leader in IDE/ATA technology, which peaks at 133MB/sec. The next version of SATA will hit 300MB/sec, followed by 600MB/sec, and possibly onwards and upwards from there.

Now this is all good stuff and much to be welcomed. However, the fact is that hard drives themselves are not yet sufficiently speedy to make the most of this new interface. Raw performance benefits are thus largely theoretical for now.

That said, if your motherboard currently has an IDE/ATA/33 or 66 interface (i.e. with a data throughput of only 33 or 66MB/sec, see the Speed #2 section on p53) and you intend to install a new hard disk, you might want to upgrade to SATA. This is easily achieved with a SATA expansion card. This gives you a couple of SATA sockets on a circuit board that slots into a spare PCI expansion slot on the motherboard. Even if you see no real-world benefits, you will at least have a SATA drive that could be reused in a future system. IDE/ATA drives may soon be obsolete and the motherboards of tomorrow will lack suitable sockets, so buying SATA now brings with it a spot of future-proofing.

On a point of interest, or at least note, the PCI socket itself has a maximum data throughput of 133MB/sec. This is slower than SATA's 150MB/sec throughput, so you wouldn't appreciate the full potential of the drive even if it could pump out bits and bytes at 150MB/sec. Which it can't. Again, see Speed #2.

There are two other advantages of SATA over IDE/ATA. First, the interface uses a much narrower cable than the flat, wide, ribbon-like IDE/ATA design. These cables are neater and easier to work with, and don't impede airflow inside the case to anything like the same extent. Secondly, because each SATA channel supports only a single drive, there is no need to daisy-chain drives on the same cable or worry about jumper settings.

There is no channel sharing with Serial ATA: one drive per cable and socket.

TECHIE CORNER

IDE/ATA standards Just one IDE/ATA standard? That'll be the day! Here's a summary of the main specifications in the order in which they appeared. Forget what they mean, how they evolved and why they matter: when buying a new drive, just make sure you choose one that matches your motherboard's particular flavour of IDE/ATA support (time to check that manual again). Or check the stickers on your existing drives and buy like for like.

IDE	ATA-1
EIDE	Fast ATA-2
EIDE Ultra33	ATA/33
EIDE Ultra66	ATA/66
EIDE Ultra100	ATA/100
EIDE Ultra133	ATA/133
ATAPI	An IDE standard that supports devices other than hard disks, such as CD-ROM and DVD drives.

Oh, and ATA is sometimes called DMA (or UDMA) instead.

Internal versus external drives

You don't need to open up your PC or worry in the slightest about sockets if you opt for an external model.

An external hard drive is basically the same device as an internal model only housed in a case rather than installed in a drive bay. It needs to connect to the motherboard, of course, but your computer doesn't have any accessible IDE/ATA or SATA sockets on the outside of the case. Therefore, an external drive hooks up with the rest of the system through either a USB or a FireWire port (or, rarely, via an external SCSI interface but we won't worry about that here). External drives are thus only really an option if your computer has a USB 2.0 or FireWire interface, but we'll show you how to add this later.

External hard disks are portable, practical and probably not as pricey as you might imagine.

Pros and cons

External drives are always a little more expensive than their internal counterparts as you pay for a protective case, a button or two and perhaps a panel of blinking lights (for which read, external drives can be something of a rip-off). However, the advantages are truly considerable. An external drive is portable, which means you can use it at home and in the office and hook it up to just about any PC anywhere. Some are bulky as bricks but offer tremendous capacity, while others fit in your palm or pocket.

Because they simply plug into a port around the back of your PC, or perhaps into a USB hub, external drives save you the hassle of an installation routine (not that installing an internal drive is any great drama, as we will demonstrate). Most drives don't even require software drivers, so you can start using them immediately upon connection. You can also disconnect a drive at any time without having to reboot the computer. That's the joy of 'plug-and-play'.

It's always easier to find what's wrong with a device when you can see it (and give it a shake), especially if it has self-diagnostic measures built in. And it's much easier to take back to the shop if it's a DOA dud.

For large-scale backups, what could be easier? Indeed, it's perfectly possible to backup up your entire primary hard disk to an external device once a day (preferably overnight) and then carry it off for safe-keeping elsewhere. See p68.

Some drives, particularly the smaller models, are bus powered. This means that they draw the current they need to operate from the USB or FireWire socket. This in turn means no need for power cables or plugs.

As for the disadvantages… well, you can't install Windows on an external hard disk and use it to run your computer (actually, in some situations, you can but not without difficulty and complications) so an external drive is no replacement for the primary, internal disk. They are also extremely nickable, prone to get left on trains and deeply attracted to coffee spillages.

External drives connect via USB (left) or FireWire (right). In terms of relative performance, they are more or less identical.

This mini-drive has a whopping 20GB capacity but is powered directly through the USB interface.

PART 3

Step-by-step hard disk upgrade

As we've mentioned, you can install a new internal hard disk either as a replacement for the old one, in which case you'll have to reinstall Windows, or as an ancillary drive, in which case you end up simply with more storage space.

Virtually all tower cases have space for a second hard disk but it pays to check before plunging ahead. Also, a second hard disk should be installed on the same IDE/ATA channel as the primary disk, which means that it must share the same ribbon cable. Check that the existing ribbon cable has a spare connector. If not, you'll need to get hold of a new one. See p54 for details.

Installing a new hard disk is just the same as uninstalling an old one, although obviously in reverse. In the following example, we'll remove an existing disk in preparation for a replacement. To fit a second disk, you would simply install it in a free drive bay and make the same power cable and ribbon cable connections, being sure to use the same ribbon cable as the primary disk and remembering to set the jumpers accordingly (see Step 6).

This full-size tower case has no shortage of drive bays: three for 5.25-inch drives (typically CD and DVD drives) and no less than four for 3.5-inch drives. One of these is reserved for the floppy drive but that leaves plenty of scope for hard disk upgrades.

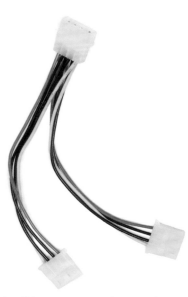

A splitter overcomes a shortage of power cables.

Before commencing any internal work on your PC, re-read the safety precautions on p33.

Make sure that you can access the drive bay. Sometimes this means removing a plastic cover on the front of the case. Also check how to secure the disk in place. Usually this is a simple case of inserting screws on either side of the bay, but occasionally a sliding rail mechanism is used instead. Begin by unplugging the four-wire power cable from the rear of the drive.

Now carefully remove the ribbon cable from the drive, leaving the other end connected to the motherboard.

Unscrew the drive from its bay...

And carefully remove the drive from the computer.

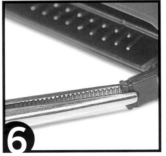

Now you need to set the jumpers on your new hard disk. This determines whether the device will be the master (or sole) device on this IDE/ATA channel, or the slave (see p54). If this is a replacement drive, it will certainly be the master; if it's a secondary drive sharing a ribbon cable with the existing drive, it will be the slave. Check the manual that came with the disk for instructions on how to set the jumpers appropriately. You may also find a jumper guide printed on the hard disk casing. Remember that you can also set the jumpers to the Cable Select position and let the cable sort out this master/slave nonsense.

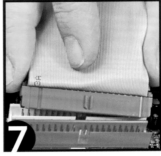

Slot the new hard disk into the vacant drive bay and reattach the power and ribbon cables i.e. reverse Steps 2–5. Be sure to match the Pin 1 stripe on the cable with Pin 1 on the drive. A secondary drive should be installed in a free drive bay close to and preferably beneath the existing drive (this makes it easier to attach the shared ribbon cable). Don't over-tighten the screws as they mustn't poke too deeply into the bowels of the drive. Also check that the ribbon cable is still securely attached to the primary IDE/ATA socket on the motherboard, or plug it in now if you're using a new cable.

TECHIE CORNER

Fat disks and FAT Quite aside from any BIOS limitations, the very first release of Windows 95 did not support the use of the FAT32 (file allocation table) file system. But the second release – Windows 95 OSR2, or just Windows 95b – did, as do Windows 98, Millennium Edition and XP. The important point is that only FAT32 systems can recognise hard disks larger than 2.1GB, which severely limits the attraction of an upgrade if you're still stuck with the original Windows 95.

Beyond FAT is NTFS, or New Technology File System, a more robust and efficient file system suitable only for Windows XP and 2000. When you install Windows XP on a FAT formatted disk, you are given the opportunity to upgrade. We recommend this.

Partitioning and formatting
the new hard disk

Before you can use your new disk, you must partition and format it. The first procedure tells the computer how many separate 'chunks' of usable space there are on the physical disk – the norm would be one, unless you want to sub-divide the disk space (see p26-28) – and the second determines which file system the operating system will use. A file system is simply a means of organising data on the disk, and your choices are FAT32 (for Windows 98 and Me) and NTFS (for Windows XP and 2000).

Now, most hard disks are supplied with their own setup software and that's very much the way to go if possible. However, you can also format and partition a disk with a Windows start-up floppy disk or the Windows XP CD-ROM. In the following example, we'll work first with a Windows 98 start-up disk and then take the Windows XP approach.

```
                 Microsoft Windows Millennium
                    Fixed Disk Setup Program
              (C)Copyright Microsoft Corp. 1983 - 2000

                          FDISK Options

     Current fixed disk drive: 1

     Choose one of the following:

     1. Create DOS partition or Logical DOS Drive
     2. Set active partition
     3. Delete partition or Logical DOS Drive
     4. Display partition information
     5. Change current fixed disk drive
```

If you see this menu in Step 4 below, be sure to type '5' to change from the primary disk (the one with Windows) to the new disk (the one that's fresh out of the box).

Please note that we are working with a single hard disk here i.e. a new drive that has just been installed as a replacement for the old. One critical note at the outset. If instead you need to partition and format a secondary hard disk – that is, a new disk installed alongside the existing disk – then you must (must!) take great care in Step 4. When Fdisk detects that there are two physical disks in the computer, it provides a fifth menu option: Change current fixed disk drive. Be sure to select this to ensure that all forthcoming operations affect only the new disk. If you don't, you could lose your existing Windows installation and all your files.

Using a Windows 98/Me start-up disk

We discussed the routine for making a Windows start-up disk back on p26-28. Here now is an opportunity to use it.

1

Enter

Insert your Windows start-up disk in the floppy drive and turn on the computer. This first step starts it running in DOS mode and affords access to the programs on the floppy. You will probably see a notice about the disk requiring formatting.

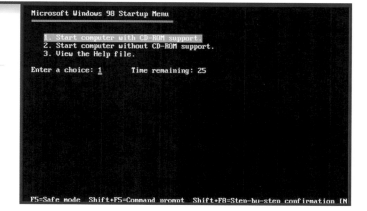

```
Microsoft Windows 98 Startup Menu

1. Start computer with CD-ROM support.
2. Start computer without CD-ROM support.
3. View the Help file.

Enter a choice: 1          Time remaining: 25




F5=Safe mode  Shift+F5=Command prompt  Shift+F8=Step-by-step confirmation [N
```

fdisk

Enter

After a minute or so, you'll be presented with a daunting, blinking prompt. Type fdisk and press the Enter key.

```
This may take a few minutes. Please wait...

Windows 98 has detected that drive C does not contain a valid FAT or
FAT32 partition. There are several possible causes.

1.   The drive may need to be partitioned. To create a partition on the drive,
run FDISK from the MS-DOS command prompt.

2.   You may be using third-party disk-partitioning software. If you are using
this type of software, remove the Emergency Boot Disk and restart your
computer. Then, follow the on-screen instructions to start your computer from
a floppy disk.
.
3.   Some viruses also cause your drive C to not register. You can use a virus
scanning program to check your computer for viruses.

The diagnostic tools were successfully loaded to drive C.

MSCDEX Version 2.25
Copyright (C) Microsoft Corp. 1986-1995. All rights reserved.
          Drive D: = Driver MSCD001 unit 0

To get help, type HELP and press ENTER.

A:\>fdisk
```

Y

Enter

Confirm that you wish to enable support for large hard disks, and press Enter.

```
Your computer has a disk larger than 512 MB. This version of Windows
includes improved support for large disks, resulting in more efficient
use of disk space on large drives, and allowing disks over 2 GB to be
formatted as a single drive.

IMPORTANT: If you enable large disk support and create any new drives on this
disk, you will not be able to access the new drive(s) using other operating
systems, including some versions of Windows 95 and Windows NT, as well as
earlier versions of Windows and MS-DOS. In addition, disk utilities that
were not designed explicitly for the FAT32 file system will not be able
to work with this disk. If you need to access this disk with other operating
systems or older disk utilities, do not enable large drive support.

Do you wish to enable large disk support (Y/N)...........? [Y]
```

1

Enter

Type 1 to proceed – or, if you have installed a secondary disk, type 5 (see p61).

```
                          Microsoft Windows 98
                       Fixed Disk Setup Program
              (C)Copyright Microsoft Corp. 1983 - 1998

                            FDISK Options

Current fixed disk drive: 1

Choose one of the following:

1. Create DOS partition or Logical DOS Drive
2. Set active partition
3. Delete partition or Logical DOS Drive
4. Display partition information


Enter choice: [1]




Press Esc to exit FDISK
```

1

Enter

Here we are creating a 'primary DOS partition' on which we can install Windows later.

```
                  Create DOS Partition or Logical DOS Drive

Current fixed disk drive: 1

Choose one of the following:

1. Create Primary DOS Partition
2. Create Extended DOS Partition
3. Create Logical DOS Drive(s) in the Extended DOS Partition


Enter choice: [1]




Press Esc to return to FDISK Options
```

Y

Enter

Fdisk now verifies the disk's integrity, which is a way of looking for physical errors like duff sectors. When it's finished, confirm that you wish to use all the available disk space. Another integrity check now commences.

```
                          Create Primary DOS Partition
Current fixed disk drive: 1

Do you wish to use the maximum available size for a Primary DOS Partition
and make the partition active (Y/N)....................? [Y]




Verifying drive integrity,  63% complete.
```

Escape

When you hit the Escape key, Fdisk will close and the computer returns to the prompt we saw in Step 2. At this stage, use the reset button to turn the computer off and back on again. Leave the floppy disk in the drive.

```
You MUST restart your system for your changes to take effect.
Any drives you have created or changed must be formatted
AFTER you restart.

Shut down Windows before restarting.




Press Esc to exit FDISK
```

---

format c:

Y

Upon restart, repeat Step 1. Now type format c: (including the colon) and type Y to confirm that you don't mind losing data. This being a new clean disk, there is of course none to lose.

```
Preparing to start your computer.
This may take a few minutes. Please wait...

The diagnostic tools were successfully loaded to drive D.

MSCDEX Version 2.25
Copyright (C) Microsoft Corp. 1986-1995. All rights reserved.
      Drive E: = Driver MSCD001 unit 0

To get help, type HELP and press ENTER.

A:\>format c:

WARNING, ALL DATA ON NON-REMOVABLE DISK
DRIVE C: WILL BE LOST!
Proceed with Format (Y/N)?Y
```

Enter

You aren't given a choice of file system here because Windows 98 and Me can only be installed on a FAT32 disk so that is the file system used automatically. Formatting now takes a few minutes. Hit the Enter key when prompted to assign a volume label. Your new disk is now ready for Windows.

```
WARNING, ALL DATA ON NON-REMOVABLE DISK
DRIVE C: WILL BE LOST!
Proceed with Format (Y/N)?Y

Formatting 16,37.73M
Format complete.
Writing out file allocation table
Complete.
Calculating free space (this may take several minutes)...
Complete.

Volume label (11 characters, ENTER for none)?

   16,362.73 MB total disk space
   16,362.73 MB available on disk

       8,192 bytes in each allocation unit.
   2,094,429 allocation units available on disk.

Volume Serial Number is 1A7B-15D8

A:\>
```

d:

 setup

 Enter

To install Windows, restart the computer once more and repeat Step 1. Be certain to select option 1: 'Start computer with CD-ROM support'. Now pop your Windows 98 or Me CD-ROM in the drive. When you get to the A: prompt, type d: to access the CD-ROM drive (you may need to use e: if you have two CD/DVD drives). When the prompt changes, type setup to launch the Windows setup program. The rest is plain sailing.

```
D:\>a:
A:\>d:
D:\>setup
Please wait while Setup initializes.
Setup is now going to perform a routine check on your system.
To continue, press ENTER. To quit Setup, press ESC._
```

Using a Windows XP CD-ROM

It's all a bit simpler if you have a Windows XP CD-ROM and want to install it on your new hard disk. The important thing is making sure that your computer can boot from the CD-ROM drive, which may require a BIOS tweak (see Appendix 1). When your new disk is installed – again, we are working here with a *replacement* hard disk, not a secondary disk – place the XP CD in the drive and start your computer.

 Enter

The Windows Setup program should launch immediately and beaver away on its own for a few minutes in preparation. Eventually, you'll be asked what you want to do. Just press Enter to proceed.

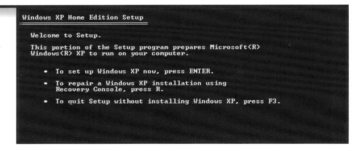

```
Windows XP Home Edition Setup

   Welcome to Setup.

   This portion of the Setup program prepares Microsoft(R)
   Windows(R) XP to run on your computer.

       •  To set up Windows XP now, press ENTER.

       •  To repair a Windows XP installation using
          Recovery Console, press R.

       •  To quit Setup without installing Windows XP, press F3.
```

 F8

 Enter

Hit F8 to agree to the license terms. If you're using an upgrade rather a full version CD-ROM, you'll have to prove your entitlement at this point. All you have to do is remove the Windows XP CD, place your old Windows disc in the drive, and press Enter.

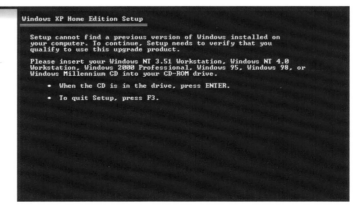

```
Windows XP Home Edition Setup

   Setup cannot find a previous version of Windows installed on
   your computer. To continue, Setup needs to verify that you
   qualify to use this upgrade product.

   Please insert your Windows NT 3.51 Workstation, Windows NT 4.0
   Workstation, Windows 2000 Professional, Windows 95, Windows 98, or
   Windows Millennium CD into your CD-ROM drive.

       •  When the CD is in the drive, press ENTER.

       •  To quit Setup, press F3.
```

Enter

The Setup program now identifies the new disk and invites you to install Windows. Press Enter to continue.

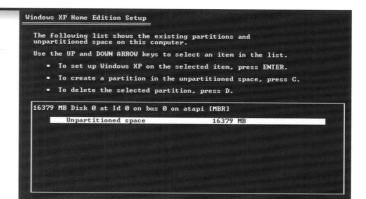

Enter

Here you can choose which file system to format the drive with. The default – NTFS – is best for Windows XP, so hit Enter. You could choose to select the 'Quick' option but this bypasses an important check on the disk's physical integrity so we wouldn't recommend it.

You'll be prompted to replace your Windows XP CD-ROM now if you had to remove it in Step 2. When the formatting is complete, the setup routine continues and Windows is installed.

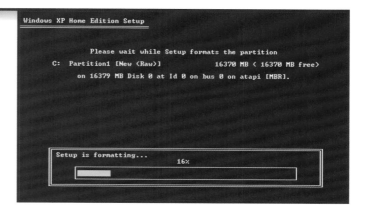

PART 3

Partitioning, disk imaging and dual-booting

Whether you have two hard disks or just one big one, there are plenty of options that go beyond mere data storage. We've already mentioned the possibility of a RAID setup (p55), although we rather suspect that few of you would bother with that. Here, though, are some further examples of useful things to do with a hard disk or two. First, the technicalities, then the practical applications.

Partitioning a hard disk

To 'partition' a hard disk is to split it into two or more independent sections that the computer treats like physically distinct disks. Each partition has its own drive letter, and each can hold data or an operating system.

Windows comes with its own DOS-based partitioning utility called Fdisk, as we have just seen. However, as Microsoft points out: 'You should not use this tool unless you are very familiar with the process of partitioning a hard disk.' Quite. Moreover: 'When you run the Fdisk command to create, delete, or change a partition, all of the data on that partition is permanently deleted.' What this boils down is that Fdisk is fine for creating partitions on a brand-new hard disk or for scrubbing a disk clean and starting again from scratch, but it's not at all suitable for creating new partitions on an otherwise healthy computer. Instead, we'd recommend using a specialist partitioning program like Partition Magic from Symantec: **www.symantec.com/region/reg_eu/product/spm_index.html**

Even here, the process is not exactly intuitive but you can create, delete, copy, merge and otherwise manipulate partitions without loss of data. That said, you should always make a complete backup of all your important files before running any partitioning software on your hard disk – just in case.

This computer actually has four hard drives but you can see that Disk 2 has been partitioned.

The same computer seen through the eyes of Windows. Now there are effectively five hard disks. Drive letters G and H relate to the partitioned Disk 2.

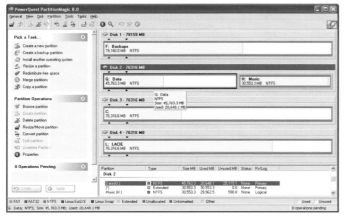

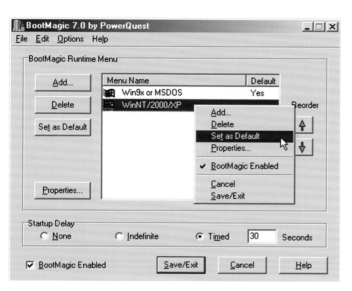

A boot manager lets you swap between operating systems.

Make life easy with a partitioning utility.

What you need to know

The language of partitioning is dense and confusing, and it seems that every possible action is subject to dozens of qualifiers. While utilities like Partition Magic provide wizards to simplify common tasks, it is still advisable to understand the basic principles and terminology. Here is a very potted guide to the basics.

Master Boot Record A vital file that tells your computer where on the hard disk to find the operating system. Without this record, it would be unable to start, or boot. The MBR also includes details of any disk partitions.

Boot manager A program that lets you swap between partitions in order to run multiple operating systems on one computer. A good boot manager kicks in every time you restart and offers a choice; less flexible versions must be configured from within Windows before closing down. Windows XP has its own built-in but rudimentary boot utility.

File system The File Allocation Table, or FAT, is a record of every file's location on the hard disk. This in turn depends upon the rules of the file system. As disks have grown in size, file systems have adapted and improved, and newer operating systems are designed to take advantage of these developments. The main file systems for Windows are as follows:

File system	Appropriate for
FAT	Windows 95a
FAT32	Windows 95b; Windows 98; Windows Millennium Edition; Windows 2000; Windows XP
NTFS	Windows 2000 (recommended); Windows XP (recommended)

You choose which file system to use whenever you create a new partition. Note that Windows 98 and Me cannot 'see' NTFS partitions, whereas 2000 and XP are backwards-compatible with FAT32.

Partition types Ancient computer wisdom decreed that a hard disk may have a maximum of four partitions. These are called the 'primary' partitions, and you can install a separate operating system on each. However, it's possible to cheat by turning a primary into an 'extended' partition, which may then be split into several 'logical' partitions. The really important point is that only primary partitions are bootable, so logical partitions are suitable for files and applications but not operating systems.

Disk imaging

A disk image is an exact copy, or clone, of a hard disk or a disk partition: an uber-backup that encompasses every last bit and byte of data in a single file, including Windows. But why is that important?

Well, with a normal backup you copy files and folders. In the event of disaster – the theft of your computer, say, or total hard disk failure – you can at least recover your work. So long as you still have your original Windows and program discs, you can also start afresh on a new PC or hard disk. It's a drag, though: reinstalling Windows and all your software and then setting everything up the way you like it once more can take an age. But with an image of your C: drive (or partition), you could reinstall everything at a stroke: Windows, software, settings, files, folders, the works.

The one restriction is that you must save the image file somewhere other than on the disk that it is currently being imaged, if you see what we mean. That is, you can't save an image of the C: drive on the C: drive itself.

Options include saving the image directly to recordable CDs (lots of them, probably) or recordable DVDs (fewer will be required) or to a separate hard disk, be it internal or external. However, if you have only the one hard disk but it is less than 50% full, you can partition it into two chunks and use the new partition as the storage location for an image of C: drive.

As a for instance, let's imagine you have a 30GB hard disk

This hard disk is only around a third full so there's plenty of scope to split it in two. You could then image the C: drive directly to the new partition.

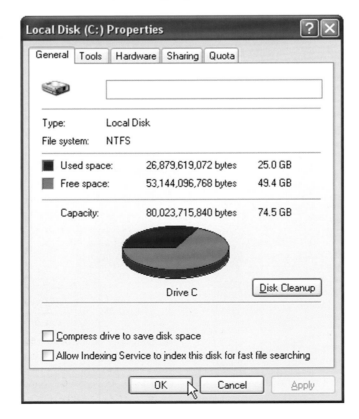

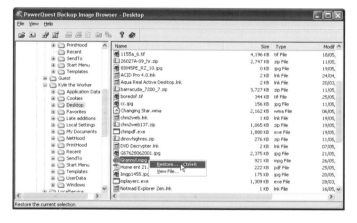

You can restore files and folders
selectively from a disk image as
well as recovering an entire disk
or disk partition in one go.

that's one-third full. You could split this into two 15GB partitions.
This gives you a new 15GB drive (D:) that's plenty big enough to
hold an image file of the existing C: drive. It also gives you 5GB
of disk space left to play with on C: drive itself.

The drawback, of course, is that the original and the image
exist on the same physical disk so if it goes up in smoke or out
the door, you'll have no recovery route. Saving image files away
from the computer is altogether safer.

Windows itself cannot do disk imaging so this is one occasion
where you'll need a third-party utility. The best, we think, is Drive
Image, again from Symantec (but formerly developed by
PowerQuest). Unlike most imaging utilities, this lets you image
the C: drive while Windows is still running, i.e. without restarting
the computer and dropping into DOS mode. It can also be
scheduled to run at regular intervals so you might, for instance,
configure it to image C: drive every night at 3am. This way, you'll
always have a fresh – and complete – backup to hand.

One other bonus is being able to copy the entire contents of a
hard disk from one device to another. This is ideal if you want to
replace an existing disk with one with a larger capacity but don't
want to have to start afresh with Windows, application software
and files and folders. Drive Image lets you transfer an image of
one disk onto another. In effect, this means that you can install a
new, large hard disk and carry on exactly as before with virtually
no disruption. However, do bear in mind that it's just as easy to
install the new disk as a second drive and leave the original disk
in place. You get all of the benefits of increased capacity with
none of the hassles. The only pressing reason to ditch the old
drive would be poor performance – perhaps it's an old 33MB/sec
model and you want to upgrade to 100MB/sec or SATA – or if
you suspect impending hardware failure.

Dual-booting

When you have two or more hard disks or disk partitions, you
can run two or more operating systems on your computer. This is
the perfect way to try out an alternative to Windows, such as
Linux, or to experiment with a new version of Windows. You may
be thinking about upgrading to Windows XP but you're unsure
whether it's really for you. After all, lots of old software doesn't
run under Windows XP and some older hardware won't work
either. No problem: in a dual-boot environment, you can run
Windows XP for everyday use and switch to Windows 98
whenever you need play an old PC game, use an old printer or
whatever.

It's possible to dual- or multi-boot in many configurations but
the easiest and, we think, the most profitable route is letting
Windows XP take the strain during installation. To get started,
you'll need to create a new logical disk partition of at least 5GB
(but preferably larger). Or, of course, you can use a secondary
internal IDE/ATA or Serial ATA hard disk, in which case partition
and format it as described earlier.

This time around, you don't need to boot the computer from
the Windows XP CD-ROM. Rather, pop the disc in its drive while
your current version of Windows is running. From the opening
screen, select 'Install Windows XP'.

New Installation (Advanced)

 Next

The setup program will assume that you want to upgrade your current version of Windows. This is the last thing you want to do. Select New Installation from the Welcome to Windows Setup menu.

 Advanced Options

 I want to choose the install drive letter and partition during Setup

OK

Here, it is essential that you enter the Advanced Options dialogue and tick the box that lets you choose where Windows should be installed. Setup will now ask you a few questions about where you live and which language you want to use.

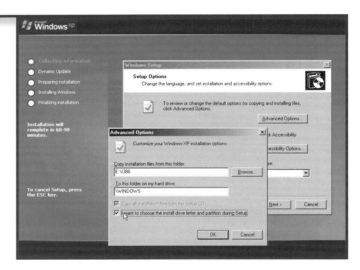

 Select new partition or new hard disk

 Enter

When you see this menu, select the new partition or disk. It will almost certainly be labelled D: unless you have several partitions/hard disk in your system (in which case be sure to choose the correct one). The point is that you don't want to install Windows on the current C: partition, as this would overwrite and wipe out your current version of Windows.

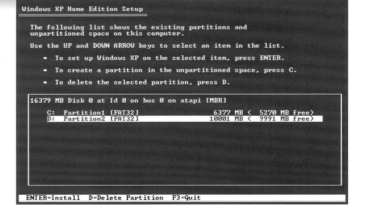

4

  Format the partition using the NTFS file system

  Enter

You'll now be presented with the format options that we saw on p65. Again, use the arrow keys to scroll down to the NTFS option. Setup will now complete the installation of Windows on the new partition or disk.

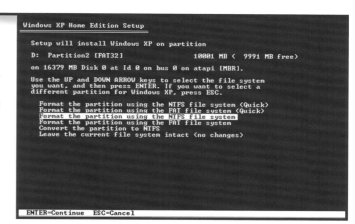

5

  Windows XP

When, finally, the computer restarts, you will see the multi-boot menu. Indeed, you will see this every time you restart in the future. You can now choose which version of Windows you wish to work with. Note that the new Windows XP installation is designated the default, which means it will start automatically after 30 seconds unless you make a manual choice. If you prefer that your old version of Windows is the default...

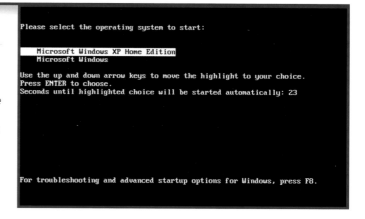

6

  Start

  Control Panel

  Performance and Maintenance

  System

  Advanced Settings

  'Microsoft Windows'

  OK

From within Windows XP, run through these steps to take control of the multi-boot menu. Here we are changing the default away from the new Windows XP installation. From now on, if left alone, the computer will eventually load the earlier version of Windows upon every restart. To start Windows XP instead, you simply have to select it from the multi-boot menu.

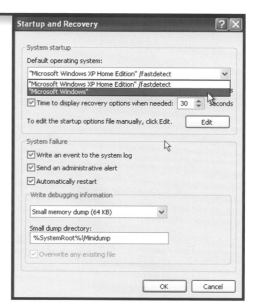

PART **3**

Upgrading to recordable CD and DVD

There are three reasons why you might consider upgrading your CD-ROM drive (apart from hardware failure, of course): to install software more quickly; to play CD-based games more smoothly; or to add extra features.

Like everything else, CD-ROM standards have evolved and today's drives are very much faster than yesterday's. Naturally enough, a fast drive can transfer data into the main computer system more quickly than a slow drive, so you'll see a big difference when you install a program on the scale of, say, an office suite. But just how often do you do that? And are you prepared to pay a good deal of money to save yourself five or ten minutes once or twice a year? We rather suspect not.

Most modern 3D action games are designed to run on quad speed (known as 4x) drives, or occasionally 8x. While a faster drive certainly can't hurt, a good games machine will benefit far more from a turbocharged graphics card and super-fast processor than a mere CD-ROM upgrade.

No, the only really good reason to rip out a functioning CD-ROM drive is to add to your computer's powers. That's exactly what we'll look at here: adding a *recordable* CD or DVD drive (also known as CD and DVD writers). Let's look at the CD option first.

A recordable CD drive gives you better backup options – and makes audio and video CDs to boot.

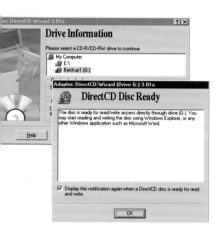

Packet writing software lets you fill a CD in bits and pieces rather than all at once.

CD writers

A CD-ROM drive can read data stored on standard CD-ROM discs such as those used to distribute software programs. It can also read audio CDs and relay the signal to a sound card in order for your PC to play music. What it expressly cannot do is record data onto a disc. For that, you need either a CD-Recordable (CDR) or a CD-Rewriteable (CD-RW) drive. The difference is simply this: CD-R drives use discs that can be recorded on to once and once only, whereas CD-RW drives use discs that can be rerecorded many times over. In fact, a CD-RW drive also works with CD-R discs, making it by far the better buy. It's been quite some time since we saw a CD-R only model on the market.

A single recordable disc holds at least 650MB of data – that's a massive 450 times more stuff than fits on a floppy disk – so the potential for archiving old files and making critical backups should be clear. Furthermore, with the right software it's easy to record your own audio compilations that can be played on household stereo equipment (note that some older car stereos won't play CD-R audio CDs) or copy existing CDs as long as you don't infringe copyright. You can even make video CDs that can be played in a domestic DVD player and watched on the television screen.

Drive	Media	Pros	Cons
CD-ROM (read-only memory)	Reads any standard CD-ROM or audio disc. Will also read 'finished' CD-R discs and *may* read CD-RW discs (no guarantee)	Essential equipment in any PC	Can not record (save) files onto disc
CD-R (recordable)	As above but also records on blank CD-R discs. These discs can be filled in a series of distinct sessions or piecemeal using packet writing software	Ideal for backing up and archiving data, copying discs and making audio and video compilations	Once full, a CD-R disc can not be re-recorded
CD-RW (rewriteable)	As above but records on both blank CD-R and reusable CD-RW discs	Maximum flexibility as you can use CD-R or CD-RW discs to suit the task in hand	Audio CD-RW discs are not always playable on domestic stereo equipment. Older CD-ROM drives can also struggle with CD-RW discs

If you have a CD writer, Windows XP lets you copy files directly to blank discs. You can either record files immediately or add files to a CD project on a piecemeal basis and burn the disc only when it's full.

CD-R discs can be written to multiple times until they are full. However, each extra stop and start 'session' has an overhead of 13MB so it's not ideal for adding lots of little files all the time. But thanks to the minor miracle of 'packet writing' software, now you can treat a CD-R or CD-RW disc just like a giant floppy and fill it up piece by piece, file by file. You may, for instance, make a daily backup of your critical work documents. Such software is usually supplied with new drives, but Windows XP also includes native support for packet writing.

Add or replace? It's perfectly possible to install a new CD-RW drive alongside an existing CD-ROM drive but there's very little point. For one thing, any CD writer is also a CD-ROM drive, and likely to be a good deal faster than the old one. For another, replacing the drive means that you save both an IDE/ATA channel and a drive bay. This should leave you space to install a DVD writer as well (more of which in a moment). Besides which, it's just as easy, if not easier, to make a direct swap.

One exception might be if you're planning to copy CDs regularly. You might want to make backup copies of your music collection, for instance, particularly now that 'CD rot' has hit the headlines (see below). In this case, it's certainly worth having two drives in your system as this lets you quickly copy a CD from the CD-ROM drive straight to a blank disc in the CD-RW drive.

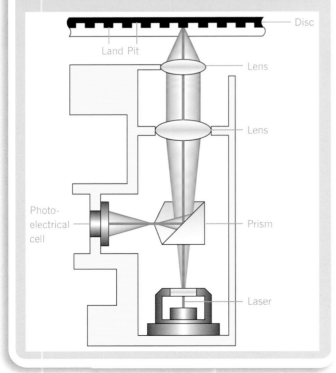

TECHIE CORNER

Optical media Broadly speaking, there are two methods of storing data long-term on a computer: magnetic media, as in the hard and floppy disks; and optical media, as in a compact (recordable or otherwise). Optical in this context means that a laser reads light patterns reflected by the disc. In a recordable drive, the laser writes data to the disc by 'burning' pits in a malleable layer. This is quite a different process to that used in industry, where compact discs are pressed rather than burned, but the effect is much the same. Incidentally, as a rule (and a perfectly silly one at that) the term disc is generally used when referring to optical media like CDs and disk when referring to magnetic media. That's the convention we're following here. For more on CD technology, start here:
www.cdrfaq.org
www.pcguide.com/ref/cd

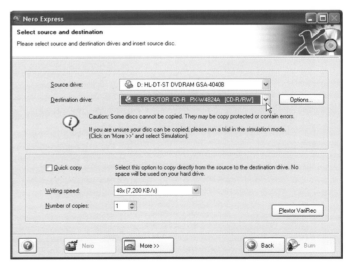

You can make an exact copy of virtually any CD with a CD-RW drive. If you only have one drive, the disc is copied to the hard disk first.

What you need to know

Praise be, recordable CD specs are nowhere near as complicated as you might expect. The critical considerations are these:

Speed A drive's speed is primarily a measure of how quickly the disc spins and therefore how quickly data is read and passed to the main system. It's a little more complicated than that – there's all that business about variable and constant velocities, seek times and access times – but let's not worry about it. The first generation of CD-ROM drives transferred data at a rate of 150 kilobytes per second, referred to hereafter as 1x speed. Later models spin the discs faster – 2x, 4x, 8x, 12x, 16x, 24x, 32x, and so on – with corresponding improvements in performance. However, 16x is generally regarded as quite fast enough for practical purposes so don't get hung up on drives claiming ludicrous and largely pointless 100x speeds.

Note that a CD-RW drive has three speed ratings: read, record (or write) and rewrite. These are usually expressed as, for example, 24x/8x/4x, which describes the drive's performance as a CD-ROM, CD-R and CD-RW device in that order. A CD-R drive has only read and record (write) speeds.

Media As discussed above, different drives work with different types of discs. CD-RW is the most flexible because it can read CD-ROM and audio discs and record on both recordable (cheap) and rewriteable (not quite so cheap) discs. However, CD-R discs offer greater compatibility and are thus better suited to audio compilations, transferring files from one PC to another and sharing data with others. Size-wise, blank discs generally have a capacity of 650MB (equivalent to 74 minutes of music) or 700MB (80 minutes) and are priced accordingly. CD-R discs are also speed rated, which means you can't use a 32x speed disc in a 56x speed drive (or rather, you can – but you have to set the recording speed at the appropriate level in your recording software).

Blank CDs are affordable and reliable. Choose the CD-R format for maximum compatibility and CD-RW for discs you can erase and use again.

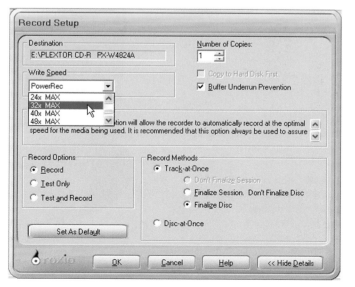

Match your recording speed to your media rating.

...and more of what you need to know

Longevity There's a good deal of passionate but not necessarily well-informed debate about which types of discs are more reliable: branded media (sometimes boxed individually; sometimes sold on spindles) or unbranded (anonymous white or silver discs, almost always sold on spindles). Well, it's certainly true that some drives work better with some discs than other, and you may have to shop around to find a perfect match. But that, we suspect, is less of a concern than it used to be. Indeed, you may well find that you can throw the cheapest of discs at your new drive and produce perfect recordings each and every time.

A more serious potential problem is longevity. You've perhaps heard the term 'CD rot' applied to audio CDs manufactured and sold in the 80s and early 90s that now no longer play. Something similar can and does affect home-burned discs. You may find that ten years down the line, or maybe five, or maybe even next year, your discs will have degraded and become unusable. And then again, you may not.

Do branded discs have a longer lifespan? Nobody knows for sure. Do CD-RW discs fare better over time than CD-R media? There is some evidence to suggest that they do. Are recordable DVDs just as susceptible to degradation? It would appear so. But the bottom line here is straightforward, although rather unfortunate: you shouldn't rely on optical media alone as a permanent archive means.

Now, it's obvious that hard disk drives can also fail, so we wouldn't suggest that you backup your digital photograph collection to a drive and forget about making a CD or DVD. The best practice is actually fourfold:

With blank discs as cheap as chips, it pays to make multiple copies of all your important files. Don't rely on just one brand, though, for you never know which discs will have the shortest shelf-life.

● Make two or more copies of your really precious files. Ideally, you should have one copy on a secondary hard disk, and another one or two copies burned to CD or DVD, preferably using two different brands of media. This way, should one optical disc rot or otherwise fail somewhere down the line, you will have one or more backup copies that may well be fine.

● Make new copies of your files periodically. If you saved your old business accounts to a CD-R three years ago, copy those files now to a fresh disc (while you still can!). That's the beauty of digital files: you can make perfect copies or original files time and time again.

● Don't store blank recordable CD and DVD media for years on end. You're better off buying discs in smaller quantities as and when you need them than digging out old discs that may already be halfway towards uselessness.

● Finally, when the successor to magnetic and/or optical media comes along, whatever it is, be prepared to transfer your files from hard disk, CD or DVD. Nothing goes stale quite as quickly as yesterday's cutting edge technology, and you could conceivably find yourself at some not-so-distant point in the future with a bunch of precious discs and, er, no surviving drive to play them on.

Interface Like the hard disk, an internal CD drive connects to the rest of the computer through a channel. This may either be IDE/ATA – in fact, a specific IDE standard known as ATAPI – or, very rarely, SCSI. As a rule, hard disk and CD/DVD drives should be kept on separate channels. If you already have two drives in your system – a DVD-ROM and a CD-RW, say – they will almost certainly share a ribbon cable.

Incidentally, you don't need the 80-wire IDE/ATA cable that we discussed on p54 for a CD or DVD drive. It doesn't hurt to use one, but it's not essential.

Drive bay Optical drives of all persuasions use the standard 5.25-inch 'half height' drive bay (see p19). Assuming that your PC already has a CD-ROM drive installed, there will almost certainly be at least one free drive bay either above or below it. In fact, most tower cases actually have three 5.25-inch drive bays so you should have an easy upgrade option even if you already have two drives – although, as we said, it's just as easy to install a new writer drive as a replacement for an old CD-ROM model.

Internal or external?
No contest: an internal drive is convenient and an external drive is fussy. Only consider an external model if you need to move the drive from PC to PC or if you really can't face an internal upgrade. An external *hard disk* drive makes sense because you can unplug it and carry around huge quantities of data; but with a CD writer the media itself (recordable discs) is portable and the hardware best left *in situ*.

Buffer stuff
If a PC fails to supply data to the drive quickly enough during a recording process, the drive temporarily runs out of work. Unfortunately, instead of pausing and waiting for the system to catch up, it throws out a ruined disc (an expensive silver drinks coaster). It's a problem known as buffer under-run and it used to be a mighty pain in the posterior. These days, though, virtually all CD writers come with buffer-underrun technology. Different implementations carry different names but the end result is the same: no more coasters. That said, you are still well advised not to do anything too taxing with your PC while a disc is being burned.

Plenty of room for expansion if your PC has three drive bays. You may need to prise off or unclip a plastic bay cover to get at the spare.

An external CD-RW drive is basically an internal drive in a tougher case with a USB or FireWire interface.

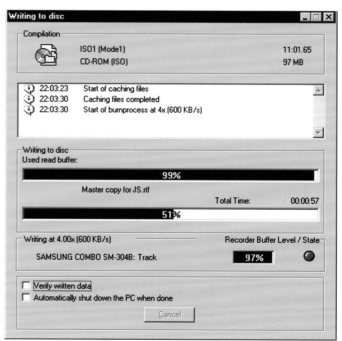

Don't play with your PC while burning a CD if you want to avoid buffer under-run.

DVD-ROM

The first D stands for Digital, the second for Disc, and the V in the middle for Versatile (not Video, though who really cares?). Essentially, DVD is another form of optical storage. The discs look just like any old CDs but with one big difference: vastly increased capacity. Anywhere from 4.7GB to 17GB, to be precise – and, yes, that means that a single disc quite possibly holds more data than your current hard disk.

The popularity of DVD is mainly due to the fact that a single disc can store and play a full-length feature film at a remarkably high quality level. Some weighty software programs, particularly reference titles crammed with film and sound clips, are also distributed on DVD.

What's more, a DVD-ROM drive (that's ROM as in read-only memory, which means it has no recording ability) can also play CD-ROM, CD-R and CD-RW discs. Some clever 'combo' DVD drives combine the recording functionality of a CD-RW drive with DVD playback so you effectively get a DVD-ROM and CD-RW drive in one unit. And some drives that are cleverer still also let you record your own DVDs, as we shall shortly discuss.

In the name of making life as simple as possible, our ever-present mantra, a multi-function drive is potentially the best upgrade of all. Why fuss with separate CD-ROM, CD-RW and DVD drives when a single device does the lot? We would temper this only with two thoughts, the first of which is the classic problem of putting all your eggs in one basket: if the drive fails, you'll be left temporarily without any means of playing audio or data CDs and DVDs. The second caveat is that two drives are handy if you want to copy CDs, as it saves the bother of having to copy the source disc to the hard drive first.

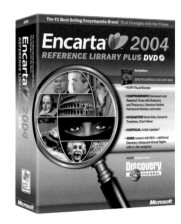

Large software programs are sometimes distributed in DVD format for convenience.

A DVD drive turns your PC into a home cinema.

What you need to know

There are several considerations before diving into DVD.

Speed DVD drives are rated in terms of how quickly they spin, just like CD drives. However, while higher spin rates (e.g. 16x) make for quicker data transfer when installing software, all movies play at 1x. Speed is thus not really an issue.

Interface Internal DVD drives use either the IDE/ATAPI or SCSI interface. Installing one is almost as straightforward as fitting a recordable CD drive. However...

Hardware acceleration Playing DVD movies on a computer demands a great deal in the way of system resources, and only a mid-range Pentium II processor or better is up to the task. This is because the video on a disc is considerably compressed and must be decompressed by the computer during playback. If the processor lags behind, the result is a jerky picture or outright failure.

All is not lost as it's possible to install a dedicated DVD decoder expansion card to take the burden away from the system processor, with the result that even humble Pentium systems can play jitter-free films. The decoder card uses a PCI slot on the motherboard and thus involves a little more surgery than fitting a drive alone. Alternatively, DVD playback hardware is sometimes provided by modern graphics cards. Such cards take much of the processing strain away from the system processor and largely eliminate the need for a separate decoder card even when paired with a relatively slow processor.

Sound A good sound card is also desirable to make the most of the high quality digital audio signal used in DVD films.

Software You'll need to install DVD playback software to watch a movie on your monitor but something suitable may come in the box with the drive. If not, it's possible to tempt Windows Media Player – the music and movie player bundled with Windows – into action. What it needs is a DVD codec i.e. an add-on software component for decoding DVD files. For full details, see the Windows Media Player website:
www.microsoft.com/windows/windowsmedia/default.aspx
Search for 'DVD' to find the correct component.

Don't forget to install a software player if you want to watch movies on your computer.

Virtually all graphics cards can handle DVD playback these day

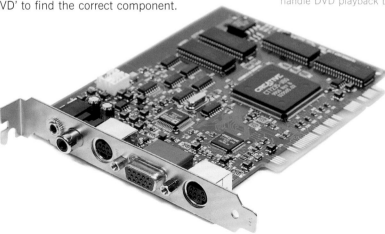

DVD writers

The issue here is one of compatibility: not all home-burned DVD discs will play on all computer DVD-ROM drives or DVD players. To muddle through this maze, you need to understand a little about the various recordable formats.

Formats explained First up is DVD-RAM (Random Access Memory). Like a hard disk drive, a DVD-RAM drive can read and write data to a disc simultaneously. This makes it ideal for specialist applications like video recording. Specifically, you can watch one pre-recorded program while simultaneously recording another. This, though, is more the meat of home entertainment than computers, so you'll commonly find RAM discs used in domestic DVD recorders of the type designed to replace tape-based VCRs.

RAM discs are rewriteable, come with or without protective covers called caddies and cost a packet. Importantly, for present purposes, they cannot be read in a standard DVD-ROM drive or played in a DVD video player. This, then, is not the format of choice if you want to share your output.

Next up are the two so-called 'dash' or 'minus' formats, pioneered by Pioneer and the DVD Forum. You will see these expressed on the page and product boxes as DVD-R and DVD-RW. As in the lingo of recordable CDs, the 'R' stands for recordable (use once) and 'RW' for rewriteable (use many times over). Virtually all drives can now burn both R and RW media, a capability usually expressed as R/RW.

The dash format is ideal for recording both data and video discs, with one traditional, significant drawback: when the first drives hit the market (-R in 1997; -RW in 1999), many DVD video players of the time could not read their discs.

So along came the breakaway DVD Alliance – original members included HP, Philips and Sony – with an alternative format known as 'plus'. Again, there are recordable and rewriteable variations, expressed respectively as DVD+R, DVD+RW and, when combined, DVD+R/RW. Recognising that recordable DVD technology would only take off commercially if people could watch their home-burned videos on a television set rather than a monitor screen, the plus format promised and delivered greater compatibility with standalone DVD video players.

Share cares So what can we say for sure about the compatibility of each format with anything other than itself? Here are the salient points:

● Most computer DVD-ROM drives can read dash and plus discs, so sharing files is usually no problem.

● All recordable DVD drives can read DVD-ROM discs. They can also read audio CD, CD-ROM, CD-R and CD-RW media. In fact, most can do CD recording as well, which is a handy bonus.

● A plus format drive can usually read a minus format disc but not record to it. And vice versa.

● Most new DVD video players can read both dash and plus video discs. Older players typically do better with the plus format, but this should not be taken for granted.

But in the end it is simply impossible to state unequivocally that any disc burned on drive Y in format Z will play on any given device or in any given drive.

The DVD Alliance introduced greater compatibility with the DRD+R and RW formats.

The DVD Forum represents companies that develop and sell 'dash' or 'minus' format DVD hardware.

Fancy making movies? A DVD writer gets your masterpiece off the PC and onto a DVD.

A multi-format DVD writer is the way to go, we reckon. This model is cheap, easy to install and use, and handles anything you throw at it.

Which DVD for me? Choosing a DVD writer rather depends on your starting point. For instance, if you only intend to make discs for use on your own computer, any format, even DVD-RAM, will suffice. However, do consider that one day you might need to access your discs on a different system. For example, your computer may be stolen and you may have to reinstate backups on its replacement. This makes dash or plus a safer bet, as you wouldn't have to shell out for another RAM drive.

If you already own a DVD video player and intend to make movies, find out which formats the player supports and shop for a drive accordingly. If the manual doesn't make this explicit, a little online research should help (Google is your friend). Alternatively, if you already own a recordable drive, be sure to buy a DVD player that can cope with its output. As noted above, most new players handle all formats perfectly.

Better still, sidestep compatibility concerns with a multi-format drive. There are three types to choose from:

● DVD-RAM & DVD-R/RW   Dash and RAM formats combined

● DVD±R/RW   Dash and plus formats combined

● DVD±R/RW & DVD-RAM   All five recording formats in one device.

On the principle of increasing your options, the last of these has to be the one to go for. Incidentally, while Microsoft backs the plus format on grounds of technical superiority – specifically, it is almost as well suited to drag-and-drop recording as DVD-RAM – the next generation of Windows, Longhorn, will support all DVD recording formats.

Here's a summary of which drives can read and record to which CD and DVD formats.

Device (read/record ability)									
		DVD-ROM drive	DVD-R/RW drive	DVD+R/RW drive	DVD-RAM drive	DVD-R/RW & DVD-RAM drive	DVD±R/RW drive	DVD±R/RW & DVD-RAM drive	DVD video player
Recordable media format	DVD-R/RW	read (usually)	read/record	read (usually)	read (usually)	read/record	read/record	read/record	read (usually)
	DVD+R/RW	read (usually)	read (usually)	read/record	read (usually)	read (usually)	read/record	read/record	read (usually)
	DVD-RAM				read/record	read/record		read/record	
	DVD-ROM	read	read	read	read	read	read	read	
	CD-ROM	read	read	read	read	read	read	read	
	CD-R/RW	read	read/usually record	read/usually record	read	read/usually record	read/usually record	read/usually record	read (usually)

Step-by-step CD/DVD drive upgrade

Installing an optical drive is easy and it makes no difference whether it's ROM or RW, or CD or DVD. The key things are remembering to set the drive jumpers – when two devices share an IDE/ATA channel and ribbon cable, one must be the master and one the slave – and connecting the cables correctly. There is also the slightly fiddly business of running an audio cable between the drive and the sound card.

In actual fact, most modern CD and DVD drives can dispense with this cable and send an audio signal through the IDE/ATA cable. Look for 'Digital Audio Extraction' support in the spec. Even if it's not mentioned, there's every chance that your new drive will play audio just fine without a direct connection to the sound card.

However, it does no harm to use an audio cable if one is supplied. Most drives have two output sockets – digital and analogue – and which you use depends upon which type of input your sound card has (or motherboard, if the audio is integrated and you don't have a sound card). If you have neither a sound card nor a motherboard with an integrated audio chip, perhaps now would be a good time to skip ahead to the sound card section!

We'll proceed here on the basis of replacing one drive with another. If you are adding a second drive, simply snap off, prise off, unclip or unscrew the nearest drive bay cover to gain access to a free 5.25-inch drive bay. Also check that the old drive's ribbon cable has a spare connector within reach, or replace it if not.

   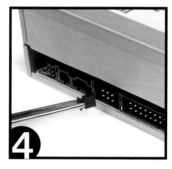

Before commencing any internal work on your PC, re-read the safety precautions on p33.

First, disconnect the existing drive. Unplug the power cable, the ribbon cable (but leave this connected to the motherboard) and, if present, the audio cable that runs to the sound card or a socket on the motherboard.

Drives are usually secured in the bay with four short screws. Remove these now to free the device and slide it out of the case.

Before installing the new drive, check the jumper settings. If this is to be only drive on the secondary IDE/ATA channel (the hard disk should be connected to the primary IDE/ATA channel), it should be set to master. However, if this drive will share a channel and cable with an existing drive, it should be the slave. Again, you can use Cable Select positions if, and only if, you are using an 80-core IDE/ATA cable (see p54). Check the documentation that came with the drive if it's not clear how to set the jumpers.

5

Slide the new drive into the bay and secure it in place with the screws you removed earlier. Be sure that the fascia is flush with the front of the case.

6

Here we see the internal connections that must be made to the rear end of the drive. From left to right: audio cable, to connect to the sound card or motherboard socket; ribbon cable, to connect to the secondary IDE/ATA channel on the motherboard (note the striped edge that designates the Pin 1 position); and power cable.

7

Here, the audio cable is being connected to the CD input on the sound card...

8

And here we are plugging it into an audio input on the motherboard. You will do one or the other, depending on whether your computer has a sound card. If it does – and even if the motherboard also has an integrated audio chip – you will take the sound card route.

9

In this example, we can see two optical drives installed in neighbouring drive bays. Note the shared ribbon cable. This connects to the secondary IDE/ATA channel on the motherboard. Once again, we must stress that optical drives and hard disks should be connected to different channels.

TROUBLE-SHOOTER

Your new drive should 'just work' when you restart Windows. However, it will probably have come with some application software, including a CD or DVD recording program, and you should install this immediately.

● If your new drive refuses to play an audio CD – and your old one worked just fine – check that the internal audio cable is correctly connected. It's a fiddly little thing that can easily be missed. See Steps 7 and 8.

● If repeated buffer under-run threatens your sanity and you

have more coasters than cups, try getting the drive to record at less than its top speed. This usually solves the problem. Also leave the PC well alone while it's busy recording. Doing anything else at the same time drains memory and increases the likelihood of under-run.

● In Windows XP, check that the drive has been enabled for recording. Open My Computer, right-click the drive icon and select Properties. In the Recording tab, check the box labelled 'Enable CD recording on this drive'.

PART 3 Floppy drive replacement

Ah, the good old floppy drive. Slow as a sloth and capable of storing a paltry 1.44MB of data per disk, it's still a staple component in virtually every PC. The drive isn't something that you'll *upgrade* as such – there's only one standard and it's not getting any better or faster – but just occasionally a drive may call it a day and need replacing. You may be tempted not to bother, figuring that you use the thing so rarely that it's not worth the bother, but a quick re-read of p25 should help change your mind. Should Windows go all peculiar, the first place you'll turn to is your start-up disk – which, without a working drive to read it, is about as useful as a chocolate teapot.

The much-maligned floppy drive is still an essential in most computer systems.

That said, if you are a Windows XP user, you should be able to start your computer with the Windows XP installation CD-ROM so long as you have a bootable CD-ROM drive and the original CD-ROM. If not, or if your CD-ROM drive itself is faulty, you may need a special set of Windows XP start-up floppies. This might be your only way to access files and folders or to reinstall a fresh copy of Windows should your existing version become corrupted. The relevant start-up files can be downloaded from this web page:
http://support.microsoft.com/default.aspx?scid=kb;[LN];310994
A floppy drive may be yesterday's technology but it still deserves a place in most PCs. Interestingly, while some manufacturers have stopped including floppy drives as standard, most new motherboards still feature a floppy drive connector.

Can you really 'upgrade' a floppy drive?

Not as such, or at least not in any meaningful way. The floppy drive requires a 3.5-inch drive bay, has a dedicated channel on the motherboard, uses a special ribbon cable with a twist and costs next to nothing. However, there are floppy drives around that include multi-format media card readers. This, we suggest, is the perfect way to upgrade a flaky floppy drive: as well as reading floppy diskettes, such a drive can read CompactFlash, SmartMedia and other forms of memory card commonly used in digital cameras and handheld computers. We'll install one such model here.

However, do note that these drives require two internal connections: the standard floppy interface and a USB interface (the latter is required to pull images and files from the memory cards). Only consider an upgrade of this description if your motherboard has a free internal USB socket (see Step 6).

This 'media drive' handles solid state memory cards as well as floppy disks, and so requires a USB connection to the motherboard. In this case, the black USB cable is hard-wired to the drive.

1 Before commencing any internal work on your PC, re-read the safety precautions on p33.

2 The existing floppy drive will have two internal connections: a power supply cable and a ribbon cable connected to the floppy drive controller on the motherboard. This socket is usually sited near the IDE/ATA sockets we saw earlier. Unplug both of these from the drive – note the peculiar split and twist in the ribbon; and note too that the power connector is smaller than the one used with the hard disk and CD/DVD drives – but leave the ribbon cable connected to the motherboard unless you intend to replace it.

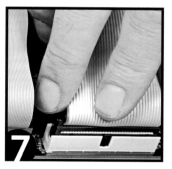

3 The drive is secured in the bay with four short screws, two on either side. Remove these and set them aside, and slide the drive forward until it's free. Occasionally, a 3.5-inch drive may be installed in a 5.25-inch bay, in which case there will be a mounting mechanism of some description. Make sure you can replicate the procedure with your new device.

4 You may find that the ribbon cable can reach through the vacant drive bay to the outside world, in which case it's easier to connect it to the back of your new drive outside the case.

5 Slide the drive into the drive bay and secure it in place with the four screws you removed earlier. Ensure that the front of the drive is flush with the case fascia. Reconnect the internal ribbon and power cables, being sure to match the striped edge of the cable with the Pin 1 position on the drive (usually the left side of the socket).

6 Because this drive is also a media card reader, we have to connect it to a USB socket on the motherboard.

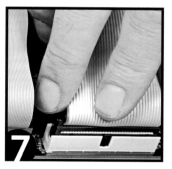

7 If you are replacing the cable – never a bad idea when changing a drive – connect it to the floppy controller interface. Note that the twisted end of the cable goes to the drive and the plain end to the motherboard.

8 Floppy drives work without special drivers and this media drive is also ready to start reading memory cards straight out of the box. With the installation complete and the case bolted back together, we can start transferring images from a digital camera's memory card to the PC's hard disk.

4

PART **4** Expansion cards

After decades of hardware evolution, today's PC has emerged with a plethora of different standards and interfaces, counter-intuitive design standards and an acronym soup of a language that purports to make 'sense' of it all. But not to worry: upgrading an expansion card remains one of the most effective ways to revamp a crusty old computer. It's easy when you know how – so let's go find out.

PART 4 A word about architecture

Today's motherboards continue to combine historical standards with the latest and fastest interfaces, but ISA is now virtually extinct.

As we have seen, the motherboard is the central component in your PC system, so much so that everything else connects to it one way or another. An interface is simply a gateway through which any two components or devices can 'talk' to each other. We've looked already at how internal drives use the IDE/ATA interface, talked about slots and sockets for processors, and plugged extra memory straight into the motherboard. Now let's turn to expansion cards.

Get slotted

Expansion slots are connectors on a motherboard used for attaching printed circuit boards (cards). The beauty of such a system is that you can immeasurably improve the performance of your computer without wielding a soldering iron. There are three main expansion slot standards (in order of age):

ISA (Industry Standard Architecture). ISA slots are black, long, slow and all but obsolete. You're most likely to find a modem in one. Or dust. You may have a couple inside your case but certainly won't find them on new motherboards.

PCI (Peripheral Component Interconnect). The PCI standard is faster than ISA and its slots (white, short) typically host sound cards, older graphics cards and perhaps a TV tuner. A USB or SCSI card can also be bolted on through the PCI interface to give a computer still more interface options. Three slots is an acceptable minimum, four better, and more are always welcome.

AGP (Accelerated Graphics Port). This is a slot designed exclusively for modern graphics cards, specifically optimised for 3-dimensional effects and digital video. There is only ever one AGP slot per motherboard, and you'll only find it on Pentium II systems and above. However, a modern machine is no cast-iron guarantee of an AGP slot as some motherboards incorporate the necessary graphics chips directly within the motherboard itself.

Blank check

Expansion slots are positioned on the motherboard in such a way that one end of an installed card pokes through a slot in a panel around the back of the PC. These slots are usually covered with blanking plates but these can be easily removed. One factor to watch is that it's not uncommon for adjacent PCI and ISA slots to share a blanking plate, with the implication that you can install one or the other type of card but not both simultaneously.

Integration

We mentioned earlier that some motherboards incorporate more features than others within their own circuitry. For instance, a motherboard may or may not come with built-in audio, graphics and network controllers, which negate the need for a sound card, graphics card and network card respectively. The main attraction of this approach is price: it's cheaper to build and sell a PC with a bells and whistles motherboard than one bristling with add-on expansion cards. Because such motherboards don't require the same number of expansion slots, it's also possible to make motherboards – and thus computer cases – significantly smaller.

However, there are downsides. With fewer expansion slots, it's not always easy to add extra features. If you want to turn your PC into a television and digital video recorder, for instance, you would want to install a TV tuner i.e. a PCI-style expansion card that can pick up and record broadcast television signals. But what if your system doesn't have a free PCI slot? Your only option would be an external tuner that connects to the computer through a USB port. That's fine, but it involves an extra power supply and plug socket and will cost you more than an internal version.

There's also a concern about hardware failure. If an integrated graphics chip were to fail, how would you fare? Well, if the motherboard had a vacant AGP slot, you could simply install a replacement graphics card – and if it didn't, you'd be up the proverbial gum tree. The only way to restore pictures on your monitor screen would be to opt for a less adept PCI graphics card or to replace the motherboard.

Let's now look in some detail at three popular and worthwhile expansion card upgrades.

Blanking plates can be removed to open up access to expansion slots.

TECHIE CORNER

Bits and buses The physical path between any two computer components – in other words, the wires that make the connection – is called a bus. The speed, or width, the bus is a measure of how much data it can handle at any one time. When we say that one interface is 'faster' than another, this is simply shorthand for saying that it's capable of sustaining a higher rate of data transfer.

The ISA standard, for example, is a 16-bit/33MHz bus, which means that it transfers a maximum of 16 bits of data (a bit being the smallest binary unit i.e. a single 1 or 0) 33 million times per second. The PCI bus started life as a 32-bit standard, which made it capable of twice the workload within the same time, and has now evolved into several 64-bit variations. Although the AGP bus is also 32 bits, it runs at twice the speed of ISA or PCI (66MHz) and is thus better suited to the high demands of graphics cards where a great deal of data has be processed as quickly as possible. For (much) more on AGP, look here: **http://developer.intel.com/technology/agp**

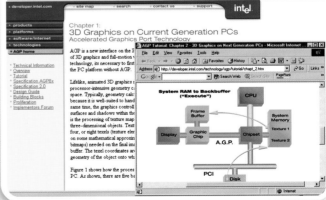

Integrated circuitry is convenient but the lack of expansion slots can make future upgrades tricky.

Upgrading your graphics card

The screenshot above shows two open windows at a resolution of 1,024 x 768 pixels; the one below shows the same windows but the resolution has been dropped to 800 x 600. Everything gets bigger, which is good for the eyes, but there's less room on screen for multiple windows.

Perhaps you want to edit digital video footage on your PC. Maybe you'd like to add a TV tuner card and use it to watch and record television. If you've developed an interest in photography, your old graphics card may be unable to display your digital snapshots in all their glory. In all these cases and more, a graphics card upgrade is likely to be a good investment.

But one word of caution: if you intend to turn your PC into a games machine then yes, you'll need a state of the art graphics card – but you'll also need a fast processor, bags of RAM, a reasonable sound card, probably a joystick, a decent monitor and stacks of free hard disk space. In many – nay, most – cases, a standalone games console may be a better bet. Indeed, a console plus a new portable television can cost less than the hardware upgrades you'll need to transform a basic PC.

That said, the popularity of computer games has been directly responsible for some remarkable technological advances and you will certainly be impressed with the performance of the latest graphics hardware if your experience of gaming begins and ends with Solitaire.

Resolving resolution Your PC's graphics card and monitor are inextricably entwined. The monitor displays the picture but the picture itself is generated by the graphics card (also called the video card). For best results, you want the card and the monitor working together to mutual advantage.

Consider the question of resolution: a measure of how much detail you see on screen. A resolution of 800 x 600 (a standard known as SVGA, or Super Video Graphics Array) means that an image is composed of 600 rows of 800 pixels (tiny points of light). A higher resolution, such as 1,280 x 1,024, equates to many more pixels and that in turn means that more information can be squeezed onto the screen without loss of detail. You might, for instance, find that you keep two or more programs open in tiled or overlapping windows rather than having to switch between them.

Graphics cards usually support many different resolutions but there is a physical limit on any given monitor's maximum display. What it boils down to is this: if you have a 15 inch monitor and don't plan to replace it any time soon, a basic graphics card that supports a resolution of 800 x 600 is all you really need. By contrast, low resolution is wasted on a 21 inch monster monitor; you'll be far more satisfied with a 1,600 x 1,200 display.

Here are the recommended optimum display settings

*Screen size **15 inch***
*Resolution **800 x 600***

*Screen size **17 inch***
*Resolution **1024 x 768***

*Screen size **19 inch***
*Resolution **1280 x 1024***

*Screen size **21 inch***
*Resolution **1600 x 1200***

What you need to know

Graphics cards are plagued with technical specifications and you need to understand at least the basics in order to make an informed purchase.

Interface As discussed earlier, graphics cards use either a PCI or an AGP slot. The big advantage with AGP is that the card can access main system RAM quickly, which avoids bottlenecks and boosts performance.

Unfortunately, if your computer was supplied with a PCI graphics card, upgrading to AGP may not be an option as your motherboard is very unlikely to have an AGP expansion slot. A new motherboard is one option here. Another is the best PCI card you can find i.e. one with stacks of onboard memory.

If your computer currently has no graphics card at all, the output is being provided by an AGP chip integrated on the motherboard. Some such motherboards provide a vacant AGP slot specifically to allow for future upgrades but many do not. If yours does, installing an AGP expansion card should automatically disable the onboard chip in favour of the new card.

Ordinarily, though, you'd swap one AGP or PCI card for another of the same type. But even here, there can be problems. The AGP interface is available in several versions that run at progressively faster speeds and so handle more data per second. These include AGP 2x, 4x and 8x. If your motherboard has a first or second generation AGP slot – AGP 1x or 2x – then installing an 8x-speed card would be a waste of time.

Furthermore, older AGP slots run at 3.3 volts whereas 4x and 8x slots run at 1.5 volts. The upshot is that you can't install a new card in an old motherboard and expect it to work. In fact, it should be impossible to do this – 1.5V cards have a differently keyed connecting edge designed to prevent erroneous installation in a 3.3V slot – but it's still well worth checking compatibility before you go shopping.

...and more of what you need to know

Memory Graphics cards come with their own slice of memory onboard. How much dictates just what it can do and how quickly. Memory also determines how many colours the card can display. If you right-click on the Windows Desktop, select Properties and click on the Settings tab, you'll see your current card's colour depth setting. If you now try to increase the setting – say, from 256 to 65,000 (16-bit) – you may find that the resolution slider automatically adjusts to a lower setting. This is because cards can typically pump out a full colour range at a low resolution or a high resolution in fewer colours, but not both simultaneously.

Memory matters. The minimum a modern graphics card offers, typically 4MB, will get you to 1,280 x 1,024 resolution in 24-bit colour and that is just fine for business work. However, you'll need 64MB or more for today's computer games.

Processor Yes, graphics cards also have processors. As you would expect, the faster the processor, the better the card is at rendering complex graphics. Look for the term 'graphics accelerator' or, for the ultimate hardware high, a GPU (Graphics Processing Unit). Add-on cooling fans are now commonplace and something of a necessary evil: we've seen, or rather heard, powerful graphics cards that display the most fantastic 3-D effects at high resolutions but sound like jet skis.

Today's graphics cards use the AGP slot and come with their own memory chips.

A cooling fan is de rigueur for a fast graphics card.

TROUBLE-SHOOTER

Never upgrade a graphics card and a monitor simultaneously. From a diagnostic point of view, you only want to work with one suspect device at a time. If Windows will only start in safe mode, the card's refresh rate is probably set too high for the monitor. Lower the setting in Display Properties. Click Start, Control Panel and Display, and look in the Adaptor tab. Your monitor probably has its own display settings, usually accessible through buttons on its casing, and you may wish to adjust the brightness or contrast to optimise the display. You can also adjust the image size to suit the viewable screen area.

Dimensions In ye olden days, graphics cards were two dimensional affairs, perfectly adequate for 'flat page' office-style work but hopeless for playing games or displaying digital video. Then along came 3-D graphics cards that sat in a slot alongside the existing 2-D model and kicked in when intensive video rendering was called for. This was clearly a daft set of affairs and so, in time, evolved the next generation of cards that combined 2- and 3-D functions. Badly. Some time thereafter, good combo cards emerged, and that's where we are today. Incidentally, 3-D isn't really three dimensional; it's just clever trickery that adds the illusion of depth to video presentations.

VGA vs DVI The very latest monitors are digital whereas the monitor currently sitting on your desk is almost certainly analogue. What happens is that your computer produces a digital signal which the graphics card then converts to an analogue signal before sending it to the monitor. This is a tad silly for it inevitably involves some image degradation, but an analogue monitor has no way of processing raw digital data. However, a digital monitor can do just this. The computer's digital images are pumped directly to the monitor in their original format and the graphics card need no longer perform an analogue to digital conversion. Look for an interface called DVI (Digital Visual Interface) on the graphics card. This may co-exist with an analogue VGA (Video Graphics Array) output or may be the only socket on the card.

You can convert a DVI output to an analogue output with a simple adapter so a digital graphics card is a good buy even if you keep an analogue monitor for now. You never know when you'll need to replace it, and your next model will probably be digital.

A simple adapter lets you connect an old analogue monitor to a new digital graphics card.

Here, the computer is connected to a TV set via an S-video TV-out connection. The red and white plugs are simultaneously feeding audio from the computer's sound card to the TV's built-in speakers.

Ins and outs As well as feeding computer-generated images to a monitor, a graphics card may have other uses. Chief of these is probably a TV-out socket that lets you connect the computer to a TV instead of, or as well as, to a monitor. If your PC has a DVD drive, for instance, or if you have saved some of your own digital video footage on the hard drive, you could hook it up to the telly and enjoy the movies on the big screen.

The two common interfaces here are S-video and composite video (see the Connectors section). It obviously helps if your TV and graphics card share the same type of interface – i.e. they both have S-video sockets or they both have composite video sockets – but it's possible to convert an S-video signal to composite, and vice versa. You can also use a SCART adapter to connect a computer to a TV that has neither. Just one important caveat: television screens are low resolution devices that are woefully unsuitable for working with a normal Windows environment.

Graphics cards sometimes also include video-in sockets, which you can use to capture video from devices like camcorders and VCRs. You can also get graphics cards with integrated TV tuners that let you watch and record live television on the PC.

Invest in a dual-head graphics card if you want to run two monitors simultaneously without having to install a second graphics card.

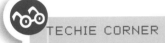

TECHIE CORNER

Display settings Changing the display settings before upgrading your graphics card can help to avert problems with Windows. If the new card's manual says something along the line of: 'change your display driver to Standard VGA', proceed as follows (note: the precise wording may vary).

1 Click Start, point to Settings, click Control Panel, and then double click Display.
2 Click the Settings tab and then click Advanced.
3 Click the Adaptor tab and then click Change.
4 Click Next, click 'Display a list of all the drivers in a specific location so you can select the driver you want' and then click Next.
5 Click Show All Devices.
6 In the Manufacturers box, click (Standard Display Types).

7 In the Models box, click Standard Display Adaptor (VGA), click OK, and then click Next.
8 Click Next, click Next, and then click Finish.
9 Click Close, click Close again, and then click Yes to restart your computer.

NB: The above instructions are adapted from Microsoft's Knowledge Base on the web and used with permission.
An alternative approach is to uninstall the original card's drivers through the Add/Remove Programs utility just before switching off the PC and installing the new card.

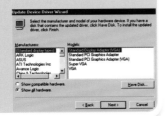

Two heads better than one?

Odd though it may seem as an upgrade option, you might like to install a PCI card alongside an existing AGP card. The point is that you could then connect two monitors simultaneously and run them as a super-wide Windows desktop. For instance, you could keep your word processor and e-mail program open in windows on one monitor and reserve the other for full-screen web surfing. Windows 98, Me, 2000 and XP all support dual monitor setups.

Alternatively, you can get dual-head graphics cards that support the same setup without requiring a separate PCI card.

Note that you can't necessarily run two monitors from a graphics card simply because it's equipped with both VGA and DVI sockets. These are often provided merely as alternatives i.e. you can use one or the other at any given time. That, however, is not always the case and sometimes you can indeed run dual monitors from such a card. Check the specs.

Step-by-step graphics card upgrade

The beauty of expansion slot architecture is that internal cards can be installed and uninstalled with virtually no effort. Here we replace one AGP graphics card with another.

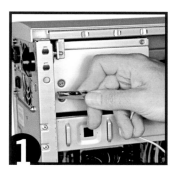

Before commencing any internal work on your PC, re-read the safety precautions on p33.

A single screw usually secures the graphics card to the case chassis. Remove this now. Support the card as you do so but try to avoid handling its components.

Many fast AGP cards are actually fairly heavy – cooling fans and heatsinks are the culprits – and so have retention mechanisms to support them in the slot. There may be a push pin arrangement or, as shown here, a clip rather like the retention clips used in RAM slots.

If present, release the retention mechanism carefully. Again, hold the card carefully and don't let it drop on the motherboard as you lift it from the slot! Remove the card from the computer case.

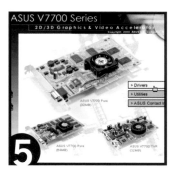

Take the new card from the antistatic bag in which it was supplied (hopefully) and reverse this procedure. Take care with the retention mechanism and be sure to screw the card to the chassis. Now carefully put everything back together, reconnect the monitor cable, and switch on the PC. All being well, Windows will automatically identify the new hardware and ask for its driver software. Pop the installation CD-ROM in the drive when prompted and follow the directions.

Display Settings can be accessed through the Control Panel or by right-clicking the Desktop, selecting Properties and opening the Settings tab. Here you can fine-tune your new display. The most important settings are screen resolution and colour depth (as discussed), and the refresh rate (see the Monitor section later). The idea here is to set the refresh rate to the highest level that the monitor supports. You should find this option by clicking the Advanced button and opening the Monitor tab.

PART 4 Upgrading your sound card

With a decent sound card onboard, your PC can eclipse your stereo in the audio stakes.

Time was when the average desktop PC emitted only feeble and occasional bleeps. But these days even the humblest domestic computer is a veritable home entertainment centre. A sound card is standard equipment in any new system, as are, unfortunately, cheap, tinny speakers that do it no justice whatsoever. More of them later but for now merely note that good speakers can enhance sound quality up to a point but the sound itself is generated internally. A powerful sound card is the starting point for aural satisfaction.

Why bother? Do you really want your PC to double as a stereo? Well, yes if you want to play audio CDs on your computer. Thanks to the phenomenal popularity of the MP3 file format and the widespread distribution (and piracy) of music on the internet, you could even build and play a music collection entirely on and from your hard disk. And then there are multimedia presentations like encyclopaedias and reference titles. And DVD movie soundtracks. And computer games. And sound files on web pages. And internet-based radio and TV channels. And so on...

Moreover, a sound card means that you can record your own music on your computer if you have the mind and/or the talent to do such a thing. Have you considered the benefits of internet telephony where long-distance calls on the internet cost a fraction of normal telephone charges? There's also the evolving world of voice recognition: speak into a microphone and smart software transcribes your words onto the page as text.

All of these examples require a sound card. The good news is that your PC almost certainly has one onboard already; the better news is that the quality and flexibility of sound technology has appreciated dramatically these past few years, yet even top of the range hardware is realistically priced. So, if your card is found wanting, give it the heave and slot in a new one.

First, of course, and as always, do a little research.

What you need to know

Figuring out which card best suits your needs is not too tricky if you keep an eye on the following considerations:

Interface Modern sound cards all use the PCI (32-bit) expansion slot. There's every possibility that your existing card is sited in an ISA (16-bit) slot but it's time to bid it a fond farewell. However, your motherboard may include an integrated audio chip, in which case you won't have a sound card at all. What you will have, at least if the chip is AC '97 compliant – an industry standard – is quite superb multi-channel sound and no pressing reason to upgrade. The only real trouble with integrated audio is that the ports are typically squeezed onto the motherboard's own input/output panel where space is tight. As a result, the microphone input may have to double-up as the centre/subwoofer output in a multi-channel set-up. What this means in practice is that you can't run a surround sound system (e.g. for music or movie playback) and keep a microphone connected (e.g. for voice recognition software) simultaneously. The port's function at any given time will be determined by the sound card's driver settings, which can be fiddly to configure.

A sound card, by contrast, usually provides a full array of inputs and outputs on the card itself and, if necessary, on an optional auxiliary port bracket or breakout box.

Incidentally, it is possible to use an external sound card. This is ideal if you're shy of opening your case, don't have a free PCI slot or want to add multi-channel audio playback to a laptop computer.

Modern sound cards use the more powerful PCI interface.

An external sound card provides multi-channel audio without surgery.

The full array of inputs and outputs on the card plus an external expansion hub (this is an alternative to a breakout box, which would require a free drive bay).

Multi-channel audio Cinema goers will be well aware of the three-dimensional 'surround sound' techniques used in today's movies, where the soundtrack comes at you from all directions. But you might be surprised to learn that you can achieve similar effects at home with a suitable sound card, especially when playing DVD movies on your computer. You'll need a whole bunch of speakers for the full effect (see p122) but there's nothing quite like it for realism.

On the other hand (there's always another hand), the vast majority of music around today was recorded in simple stereo. It's possible to 'up-mix' stereo sound into something approximating surround sound – each stereo channel is split up a bit and sent to different speakers – but results are, at best, variable. There's also the hassle factor of having to site satellite speakers all around the room. Don't underestimate this: there's no point whatsoever in connecting five (or seven) satellite speakers plus a subwoofer to your sound card unless you then position each speaker in just the right spot in your room to generate the illusion of 3-D audio. This means cables running everywhere.

Virtually all mid-range sound cards and motherboards designed with integrated audio support multi-channel output, but it's debatable just how useful this is unless you intend to spend a good deal of time watching DVD movies on your computer.

MIDI – or Musical Instrument Digital Interface – is, as the name suggests, an interface that enables a musical instrument (typically a keyboard) to connect to the sound card in order to play and record music. Or so you might think. In fact, a MIDI 'instrument' – or, more correctly, a MIDI controller – is not so different from a keyboard in the sense that it sends mute instructions to the computer. MIDI software then interprets this code and tells the sound card to make appropriate noises. Making music the MIDI way is both fabulously flexible – the MIDI file generated when you play a keyboard or other controller can be edited, modified, and applied to different sounds in an unlimited number of ways – and deeply counter-intuitive. One to master slowly, but potentially to good effect.

Many sound cards provide a MIDI interface that doubles up as a socket for a games joystick. Failing that, you can usually adapt a MIDI controller/instrument to connect via USB.

Wave table (WAV) A wave table card (see Techie Corner on p100) is essential for audio fidelity. The quality of a card's sound is measured in terms of bits, where more is better. Go for a 64-bit card if you intend to record your own music or are prepared to invest in speakers that make the most of the card's superior output; otherwise, a 32-bit card will suffice.

Duplex means that a sound card can make and record sounds simultaneously. Most conversations are duplex to some degree – we talk and listen at the same time – so a full duplex card is essential for PC chat and telephony. In fact, you'd be hard pressed to pick up a non-duplex card these days.

External connectors As we've mentioned, sound cards can provide a variety of interfaces, with or without the help of an expansion bracket or breakout box. The key considerations are:

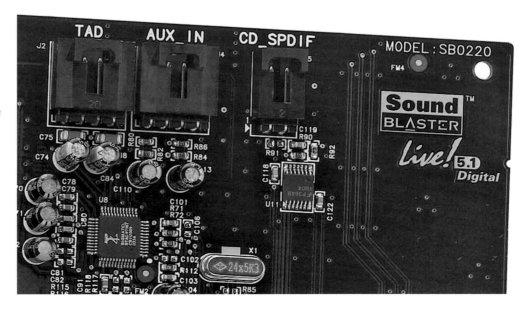

The top edge of this internal sound card includes a digital SPDIF socket for connecting to the CD or DVD drive.

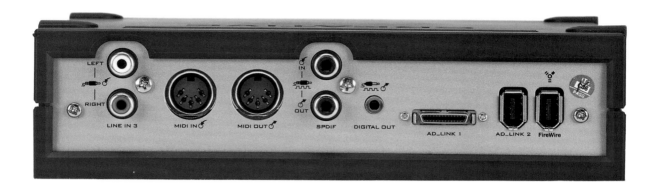

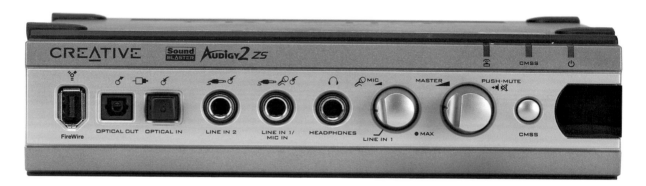

All the ins and outs you could ever wish for courtesy of an expansion hub, shown front and back. Of course, if you just need to connect a pair of stereo speakers, you can use the mini-jack connection on the sound card itself.

- *Speakers/line out* At worst, a single 3.5mm mini-jack will provide analogue stereo output. You can connect speakers here or run a cable to the auxiliary input on your hi-fi system for amplified sound. You may find three of these that together provide the six-channel output required for 5.1 surround sound (front left/right; rear left/right; centre/subwoofer).

- *Line-in* Another 3.5mm mini-jack socket that lets you connect an external device for PC recording. If you want to make a digital copy of your vinyl records or tape cassettes, for instance, you would connect your hi-fi to this input.

- *Microphone* Plug in a mic and do the karaoke. Or, in a more sober mood, use voice recognition software that transposes your spoken words into text on the page. You'll need a good quality microphone for best results and, in fact, you'll fare better with a USB model.

- *Game/MIDI* A dual-purpose interface for joysticks and MIDI instruments.

- *SPDIF* or Sony/Philips Digital Interface. A digital input/output standard. If your CD or DVD drive has a digital output, you should connect this to the digital input on your sound card. Or if your CD/DVD drive supports Digital Audio Extraction, the sound card's digital output can broadcast the audio signal directly from an audio CD (or from any file on the hard disk) without putting it through an analogue to digital conversion.

EXPANSION CARDS

Step-by-step sound card upgrade

Upgrading a sound card is just as straightforward as replacing a graphics card. Easier, in fact. In this example, we'll remove the original card from its ISA slot and install a new PCI card.

Before commencing any internal work on your PC, re-read the safety precautions on p33.

Note the thin audio cable connecting the sound card to the CD or DVD drive (or both, or neither). If present, unplug this cable at the sound card end only.

A single screw secures the sound card to the chassis. Remove this now and set aside.

TECHIE CORNER

Sampling Way back yonder, sound cards used a technology called FM (Frequency Modulation) Synthesis whereby the tone of, say, a violin was generated according to complex mathematical formulae. This worked just fine as far as it went but you'd never be fooled into thinking a Grapelli was in the room. A radically different technology called wave table synthesis was then developed. Here, actual recordings – samples – of musical instruments are digitised, stored in memory and called upon to reproduce truly lifelike music. It's still synthetic, of course, but it's the next best thing to housing a miniaturised orchestra in your PC.

Carefully remove the old sound card from its ISA slot. Hold the card by the edges and be sure not to damage its components with your fingers. This can be a fiddly business, particularly if there are other expansion cards either side, and it might take a little effort to get the card free. Do not rock it from side to side.

Take the new card from its antistatic bag and position it gently on but not in a free PCI slot. This is just to check which metal blanking plate on the chassis needs to be removed in order that the card can access the outside world.

Replace the card in its bag while you remove both the retaining screw and the blanking plate.

PART **4**

100

Gently *insert the new card in the PCI slot, making sure to match its connecting edge precisely with the slot opening. Again, be sure not to touch the card's components. If necessary, use a gentle end-to-end rocking motion to ease it into the slot.*

The idea *is to install the card fully and levelly in the slot. This will take a little downwards pressure but not enough to bend the card or crack the motherboard!*

Now *secure the card to the chassis using the screw that held the blanking plate in place or one that came with the drive. You may also care to close up the ISA slot's hole with the spare blanking plate. Anything that keeps the dust down is good.*

Reattach *the audio cables to the appropriate connector on the card (consult the manual for directions). Carefully put everything back together, reconnect the speakers and switch on the PC. All being well, Windows will detect the new card, launch the New Hardware wizard and prompt you for the appropriate drivers. Have any CD or floppy disks that came with the card to hand along with your Windows installation disc and follow the instructions.*

TROUBLE-SHOOTER

Never upgrade a sound card and speakers simultaneously! From a diagnostic point of view, you only want to work with one suspect device at a time.

● **No sound** when you play an audio CD? Did the speakers work just fine with the old card? Try plugging headphones into the CD-ROM drive (there should be a jack on the front) to make sure that both the drive and your CD playback software are working. If so, and if you have a suitable cable with 3.5mm jacks on either end, connect the headphone socket to the audio input on the sound card. If you can hear the CD through the speakers

now, the problem lies with the internal audio cable. Open the PC (after taking all the usual precautions) and ensure that it's correctly connected at both ends. Replace if necessary.

● **Just on** the off-chance, double click the speaker icon in the System Tray (the right hand end of the

Windows Taskbar) and make sure that the CD drive has not been muted.

● **Also try** playing audio files saved on the hard disk. If necessary, use the Windows Find Files tool to seek out files with the extension WAV, WMA or MP3.

● **Have a look** in Device Manager (see p23-24) and ensure that the sound card icon is not flagged with an exclamation or question mark (this would indicate a problem or conflict).

● **Modern** sound card software is often fiendishly complex. There will likely be a host of settings to play around with, probably some diagnostic tools too, and almost

certainly much less help in the manual than you would like. Look for an electronic manual on the supplied CD-ROM or consult the card manufacturer's website for further help.

PART 4 Upgrading your modem and the benefits of broadband

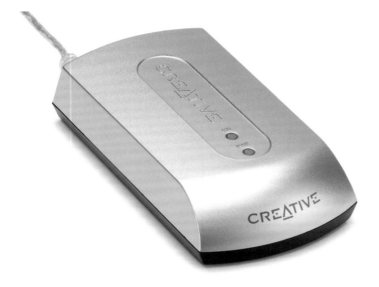

Modems come in all shapes and sizes but it's speed that really counts.

Where would we be without the wonders of the world wide web?

Modems are now a standard computer accessory. In fact, you quite possibly bought a computer in the first place precisely *because* it had a modem onboard. There may be cheaper, more convenient and in many ways better ways to get online, but the PC still provides the most common route into cyberspace.

If your current system does not have a modem, there are plenty of reasons to add one: to access email, the world wide web, newsgroups, bulletin boards and all the other areas of the internet; to send and receive (paperless) faxes; to set up your computer as a basic telephone answering machine or an advanced voicemail system. But there's only one good reason to upgrade a modem, apart from hardware failure, and that's to take advantage of the latest speeds and standards. That said, conventional modem speeds and standards have stalled and broadband is the future.

Ins and outs Although most new computers have modems fitted internally, we would strongly suggest that you consider purchasing an external modem this time around. Yes, they are slightly more expensive (although probably not as much as you'd expect) but they have several distinct advantages over their internal expansion card counterparts.

Diagnostics All external modems have an array of blinking lights that reveal what it's up to at any precise moment e.g. sending a fax or downloading a file from the internet. This makes it much easier to diagnose problems. Indeed, simply switching a modem off and back on again resolves many a headache. Just try doing that with an internal model.

Installation External modems use either a serial or a USB port. These are real, physical connections that leave little room for doubt. Internal modems, by contrast, generally sit in either an ISA or a PCI slot but use a kind of virtual port known to Windows as COM 3 or COM 4. Installing drivers and resolving problems can prove troublesome.

Convenience An external modem leaves an internal expansion slot free for another device. Remember, you only have so many slots to go around.

What you need to know

A glance at the specification sheet of a standard modem would send you to sleep in an instant. We're going to ignore the intricacies of error correction, data compression, protocols and parity because it's immensely dull and irrelevant in the current context. Here instead are the essentials:

Speed Measured in bits per second (bps). An analogue modem downloads data at a maximum rate of 56,000bps, which is why so many of us spend so much time waiting for web pages to load in our browsers. For a while, two competing 56,000bps standards called K56Flex and X2 slugged it out but neither secured total market domination and eventually they came together under the banner of the V.90 standard. This has now been superseded by the marginally improved V.92 and that's what to look for in the specs.

If your PC has a slower 28,800 or 33,600bps modem, you should see some improvement from an upgrade to V.92. Web pages will appear more quickly and large emails won't take quite so long to download. If your Internet Service Provider supports a feature called 'modem on hold', you can even pause a live connection to answer an incoming telephone call. But that's about it.

Fax A fax modem copies or emulates the workings of a standard fax machine (which is, after all, just another device that sends analogue data through the telephone line). This means that you can prepare a letter in your word processor program and fax it anywhere in the world without having to print it out and feed it through a standalone fax machine. Almost but not quite all modems can do this: look for the word fax on the box or a standard called CCITT Group 3 Fax.

Interestingly, you cannot send faxes over a broadband connection so you may wish to keep a dial-up modem installed even if you do decide to upgrade to ADSL or cable broadband. Alternatively, consider a fax-to-email service from the likes of Yac (**http://www.yac.com**). This works by providing you with a personal messaging number that you can use as a fax number quite independently of your telephone line or broadband connection. Any fax sent to that number is converted to an image and forwarded to your email address as a file attachment. You can also send faxes from your computer via email if you subscribe to Yac's premium service.

Voice A voice-enabled modem works just like an answering machine – it intercepts incoming calls, plays a recorded greeting and lets callers leave messages – but with the right software you can also set up and manage a complex voicemail service. Usually, the computer must be switched on and connected to the phone line for this to work, but some external modems are smart enough to answer the phone and take messages all by themselves.

The right software can turn your PC into a communications centre.

TECHIE CORNER

What's in a name? Modem is an acronym derived from modulator/demodulator. In a nutshell, a modem converts the digital language of computers into a series of analogue beeps and whistles that can be sent down a telephone line and converted back into digital data by a modem at the other end of the line. Typically, the other modem belongs to an Internet Service Provider which then connects you to the internet at large. Hence you get to surf the web and send email through your telephone line. It's all terribly clever – but not, unfortunately, terribly swift.

An internal modem is neater and cheaper but an external model is portable and easier to trouble shoot.

Software Modems rely on application software to do their thing. All that you need to access the internet is built into Windows but 'communications software' is designed specifically to handle fax and voice functions. Any new modem should come with at least a basic communications package in the box.

So, in summary, if you want a good modem look for V.92, fax and voice. And if you want an easy life, plump for an external model.

Installing your new modem The method for installing an internal modem is precisely the same as that for installing a graphics or a sound card: take all the usual precautions, plug it into a free PCI expansion slot, put everything back together again and restart your computer. At this point, the New Hardware Found wizard should appear and prompt you for the driver. Pop the supplied CD-ROM in its drive and follow the onscreen instructions.

The benefits of broadband

Broadband is a generic term applied to any fast internet connection. Quite how fast it has to be to qualify as broadband is moot: some ISPs now market 128,000bps or 150,000bps connections as 'broadband', while others start at 256,000bps. However, the norm is 512,000bps, or 512K. Beyond that, it's possible to get services that run twice or even four times as fast. So what does this speed mean in real terms?

Well, a 1MB file takes around 2.5 minutes to download over dial-up and about 16 seconds over a 512K broadband connection. If you want to download music or movies, that's going to make life very much easier. Even in general surfing, (most) web pages load almost instantaneously and you'll feel that the 'world wide wait' is over.

Aside from speed, there are four other tangible benefits to broadband. The first is that the connection is 'always-on'. Whereas normally you have to dial up an ISP and disconnect at the end of each session, a broadband connection is live around the clock. The beauty is that you can take internet access for granted, like just another modern convenience: sit down at your computer, and the internet is 'just there', on tap.

Secondly, broadband doesn't tie up your telephone line. This means no more missed calls and no more engaged tones.

Thirdly, broadband is usually charged at a fixed flat fee so you won't get stung with unexpectedly high telephone bills, although many dial-up internet services are also billed on a flat fee basis these days rather than the old model of pay per minute.

Finally, a broadband connection is ideally suited to sharing in a small home network. You might, for instance, set up a home entertainment-style PC in the living room, connect it to your hi-fi system, and 'stream' music files from another PC located in your study.

TROUBLE-SHOOTER

Uninstall the drivers for any existing internal modem before installing a new modem in the same expansion slot. Go to the Device Manager tab in System properties (see p23-24), highlight the modem's icon, and click Remove. Now switch off the computer, remove the old modem and install the new device. This should help ensure that Windows prompts for the new driver through the New Hardware Found wizard.

Just installed a V.92 modem and you can't connect at 56,000bps? Join the club. 56K is a theoretical speed which is seldom (okay, never) achieved in real life. This is due to various factors, including but not limited to the volume of internet traffic, the age and quality of your telephone wiring, and the mood of the gods. Connection speeds of around 40K are average and, sad to say, as good as you're likely to get without a broadband connection.

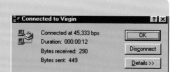

Some internal modems have two connectors on the external faceplate: one for a cable that runs to the phone socket on the wall; and one into which a telephone extension may be plugged. Failing this, you can buy a two-into-one adaptor for the wall socket and so connect both the modem and a telephone. You can't use both at once, of course – a live internet connection ties up the telephone line just like a regular call, with the temporary respite of 'modem on hold' if you have a V.92 model, a call waiting service and an ISP that supports it – but it does save fiddling around with plugs.

Most hassles are related one way or another to Dial-Up Networking, the Windows program that a modem uses to connect to an ISP. See p168 for help with common problems.

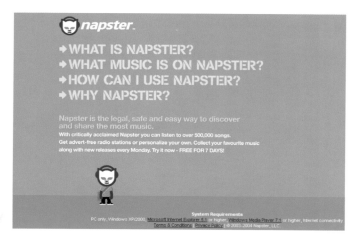

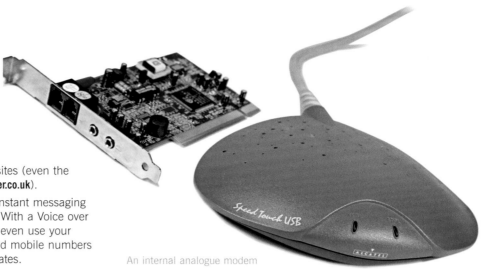

All of which means you can:

- Download music from legal distribution sites (even the infamous Napster is legit now: **www.napster.co.uk**).
- Make free PC-to-PC voice calls with an instant messaging service, headphones and a microphone. With a Voice over Internet Protocol (VoIP) service, you can even use your broadband connection to call landline and mobile numbers around the world at much-reduced call rates.
- Play online games.
- Enjoy high quality streaming video, music and radio over the internet.
- And just generally surf the web and enjoy email more smoothly.

The downside The biggest bugbear with broadband is something called contention. Your fast connection to your ISP is actually shared with several other people, potentially as many as 50 (although the figures vary). If everybody were to use the connection at the same time and, say, tune in to a high-bandwidth internet radio station, you would soon find that your own connection slowed down dramatically. In practice, this is unlikely to happen because people tend to use the internet in different ways and at different times, just as we don't all drive on the same roads at the same time. All the same, your broadband experience in the evening may be markedly slower than in the morning or middle of the night, just like rush hour on London Bridge.

An internal analogue modem and external ADSL modem side by side. The difference is more than skin deep.

Many ISPs now also impose limits on how much data may be downloaded. Although this rather flies in the face of the way we perceive broadband – a permanent, fast connection with no restrictions – the principle is that a minority of heavy users should not be allowed to hog all the bandwidth and so adversely affect the service provided to light users. Sliding scale pricing schemes are also coming into play whereby you can download as much as you like but you pay more accordingly.

ADSL and cable

There are two main types of broadband service on offer: Asymmetric Digital Subscriber Line (ADSL) and cable. The first uses your existing copper telephone line; the second is supplied through a fibre-optic cable just like a cable telephone or television service.

In the UK, upwards of 80% of us live in an area where ADSL is available and around 45% within a cabled area. However, 10% of us live beyond the reach of either. Satellite broadband is another option but it is expensive. Another option is a 'community broadband' scheme in which a single broadband connection is shared with many households, often wirelessly.

Check ADSL availability here:
www.bt.com/broadband
For cable, look here:
www.sales.ntl.com
www.telewest.co.uk

As for the installation routine, virtually all ADSL broadband services are self-install these days. Once your telephone line has been enabled for ADSL, you simply plug a 'micro-filter' into your telephone socket to split the standard voice line from the high-frequency digital signal. Connect the supplied ADSL modem, plug it into your computer, and that's that. Cable service connections usually require a visit from an engineer.

Broadband has evolved and there are speeds, services (capped and uncapped) and prices to suit just about everyone – if you can get it.

tiscali.products

Product comparison
Use this table to find out which Tiscali product is the best for you.   ☒ Close Window

	Broadbandx3	Broadbandx5	Broadbandx10 50 hours	Broadbandx10 Anytime
How much does it cost?	£15.99 a month No additional call charges	£17.99 a month No additional call charges	£19.99 a month After 50 hours then 2p per min	£24.99 a month No additional call charges
Description	Unlimited, always on Internet that's up to 3x faster than standard dial up	Unlimited, always on Internet that's up to 5x faster than standard dial up	High speed Internet access that's up to 10x faster than standard dial up	Always-on Internet access that's up to 10x faster than standard dial up.
Are there any set up fees?	£25	£25	£25	No
How fast is it?	Up to 150kbps	Up to 256kbps	Up to 512kbps	Up to 512kbps
What can I use it for?	• Faster surfing • Faster downloads • Instant email • Music downloads • Send more with your email	• Even faster surfing • Even faster downloads • Play games • Music downloads • Watch shortnews and movie clips • Sending larger files with email	• High speed internet surfing • High speed music downloads • Play challenging games & more • Ideal if you want high speed Internet but generally use less than 50 hours a month	• High speed internet surfing • High speed downloads • Watch full lengthfilms • Watch trailers and sports highlights • Music downloads • Challenging games • Live stream

PART  Adding USB and Firewire

All PCs now come with at least a couple of USB (Universal Serial Bus) ports on board and some, but by no means all, have FireWire (or IEEE-1394a, to be precise and pedantic). Both are fast interfaces ideally suited to connecting a range of external peripherals to your computer, and either can be added as a simple upgrade.

If you're wondering which interface is 'better', you're not alone. FireWire used to be much, much faster and more expensive than USB, which made it the natural choice for connecting digital video cameras to computers. However, USB then got a dramatic upgrade with the USB 2 spec (a.k.a. Hi-Speed USB) and overtook its rival. FireWire too has now been upgraded to IEEE-1394b (a.k.a. FireWire 800) which runs twice as quickly as the original interface and once again leaves USB in its wake.

USB is generally used for scanners, printers, keyboards, digital cameras, portable music players and the like. The faster USB 2 now makes it possible to hook up external hard disks and fast CD or DVD drives. FireWire is still the natural gateway for digital video – all digital camcorders have a FireWire interface – and is also well suited to external drives.

If your computer already has USB ports, we'd suggest upgrading to USB 2 if and when you feel the need for greater speed. FireWire remains a must for video enthusiasts, but do bear in mind that you'll need a very fast processor and bags of RAM to successfully edit your footage on a PC.

USB offers almost unlimited expansion capabilities. Go for the newer, faster USB 2 standard.

Check that your system can use USB before you take the plunge.

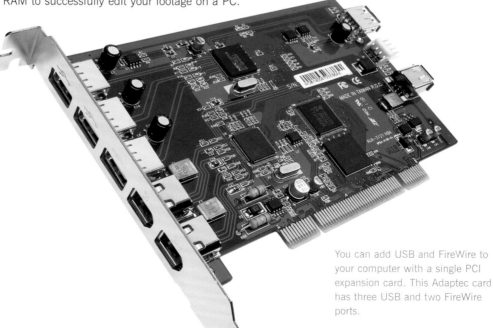

You can add USB and FireWire to your computer with a single PCI expansion card. This Adaptec card has three USB and two FireWire ports.

Perhaps the best upgrade of all is installing a combined USB 2/FireWire card. These are now readily available and open up sorts of connection possibilities in one easy, affordable move.

One small caveat: the first release of Windows 95 and everything that went before it had no support whatsoever for USB, so an operating system upgrade to at least Windows 98 and, preferably, Millennium Edition or XP is in order first. Intel has a free software utility called USBready that can give your PC a complete once over for USB readiness. Download it here: **www.usb.org/data/usbready.exe**

What you need to know

Speed An awful lot of data can pass through a USB or FireWire bus in a short time. The older flavour of USB (1.1) had a top speed of 1.5MB per second, but USB 2 runs at up to 60MB per second. Basic FireWire achieves a maximum throughput of 50MB per second, while the newer FireWire 800 standard increases this to 100MB.

Flexibility You can connect up to 127 USB devices or 63 FireWire devices to a single port, but that's more impressive in theory than in reality. While FireWire devices can be linked together daisy-chain fashion – each new device simply plugs into the last one in the chain – USB requires the use of hubs, or expansion boxes with multiple USB ports. Many keyboards and monitors come with USB hubs built in.

Plug and play Windows will (or certainly should) recognise any USB or FireWire device as soon as it's plugged in and prompt the drivers immediately i.e. no rebooting. No fussing with jumpers or other fiddly hardware settings either.

One of the most useful devices of all is a so-called USB key or flash drive. This is basically a slice of memory attached to a USB plug which you can plug into any USB port and treat just like a miniature hard drive. Perfect for file transfers and the natural successor to floppy disks.

Portable storage space with a USB drive. Available in sizes from 16MB to 1GB and beyond. Always choose a USB 2 model for speedy transfers.

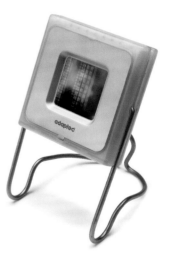

USB expansion hubs are essential if you want to connect several devices to a single port.

Hot-swappable Instead of having to reboot your PC every time you connect a device, you can plug and unplug USB and FireWire devices at will.

Just a few of the devices you can connect to a PC via USB and FireWire:

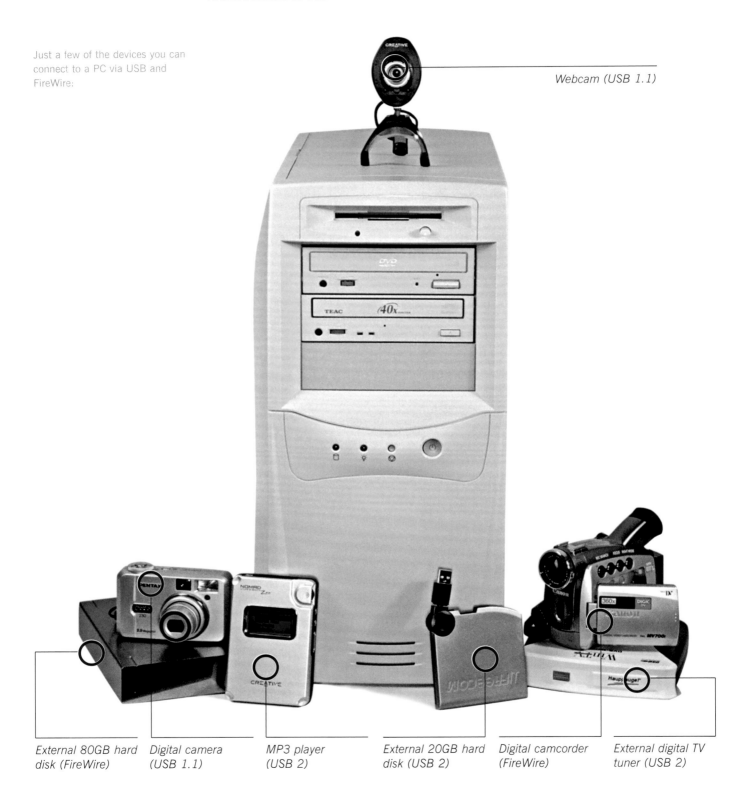

Webcam (USB 1.1)

External 80GB hard disk (FireWire)

Digital camera (USB 1.1)

MP3 player (USB 2)

External 20GB hard disk (USB 2)

Digital camcorder (FireWire)

External digital TV tuner (USB 2)

PART

Step-by-step USB card upgrade

USB controller cards typically come with two or four USB connectors and use the PCI expansion slot. Sounds simple? It is. Here's how. Note that the installation process for a FireWire card is identical.

Before *commencing any internal work on your PC, re-read the safety precautions on p33.*

Take the *new card from its antistatic bag and position it gently on but not in a free PCI slot. This is just to check which metal blanking plate needs to be removed.*

Replace *the card in its bag while you remove both the retaining screw and the blanking plate.*

TROUBLE-SHOOTER

There's nothing much that can go wrong providing you install the controller card correctly. However, here are a couple of things to look out for:

USB cables have different connectors on either end. The flatter, wider connector – Type A – goes to the USB port, and the squat, square Type B connector goes to the device. Never use a cable with Type A connectors on both ends to try to wire two computers together. For one thing, such cables are illegal; for another, you'll blow up both PCs and burn down your house.

Don't buy a USB cable longer than 5 metres. It won't work. If you really need to cover a long distance, either add a powered hub every 5 metres or daisy-chain together up to five 'active extension' cables to boost the signal.

Take out *the new USB card again and gently insert it in the vacant PCI slot, making sure to match its connecting edge precisely with the slot opening. Be sure to hold the card carefully without touching its components. If necessary, use a gentle end-to-end rocking motion to ease it into the slot.*

Now *secure the card to the chassis using the screw that held the blanking plate in place. Carefully put everything back together and switch on the PC. All being well, Windows will detect the new card, launch the New Hardware Found wizard and prompt you for the appropriate drivers. Have any CD or floppy disks that came with the card to hand, along with your Windows installation disc and follow the instructions.*

PART

Is Bluetooth worth the bother?

We look at networking proper shortly but first a few words about Bluetooth, an altogether different network technology that's been much in the news but not, we have to say, much in evidence on desktop computer systems.

Bluetooth is essentially a radio transmitter on a chip that allows various devices to 'talk' to each other wirelessly. Thus you might synchronise email and files on a handheld or laptop computer with your desktop PC, or use a cordless headset in conjunction with your mobile phone, or hook up a printer to your system without requiring a direct cable connection. These are precisely the kind of things you could do with a standard wireless network based on one of the 802.11 standards (see p145) but Bluetooth has one big advantage – and several fairly serious disadvantages.

Ups... Bluetooth's greatest strength as a networking technology is undoubtedly its low power consumption. This makes it well-suited to portable gadgets where battery life is essential. For instance, a PDA (Personal Digital Assistant, or handheld computer) soon runs out of juice when connected to a wireless Local Area Network (WLAN). However, you could use low power Bluetooth technology to connect to the same network and perform the same functions with significantly less drain on the battery. In short, Bluetooth lets you do more for longer when you're running on batteries.

And downs However, as a wireless technology, Bluetooth has one rather obvious failing: it's range is typically 10 metres or less. If your PDA was busy synching with your PC and you happened to wander a little too far from your desk, the connection would be broken. This makes Bluetooth inherently unsuitable for running an entire network except in the unlikely event that every device is located in close proximity to every other. True, some versions of Bluetooth claim a range of up to 100m but real-world experience shows this to be a tad optimistic.

Low power usage equates to longer battery life.

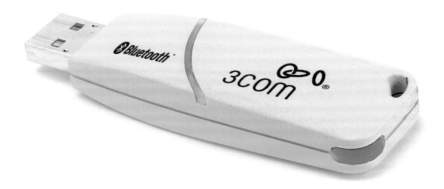

A Bluetooth adapter like this USB dongle device allows a laptop or desktop machine to join a wireless PAN.

Moreover, Bluetooth is a 'slow' technology, peaking at under 1 megabit per second. The slowest of the 802.11 wireless networking standards runs at 11Mb/sec and the fastest at 54Mb/sec, making Bluetooth a poor relation for large-scale file transfers or for streaming media.

Worst of all, Bluetooth is, or at least can be, a complete pain to configure. To get any two devices talking to one another means establishing a paired link, and this is nowhere near as easy as it should be thanks to non-standard setup routines and, especially, a lack of native Windows support for Bluetooth.

Which is not to say that Bluetooth doesn't have its uses – for synching email between a PDA and a PC or for sending images from a Bluetooth digital camera to a Bluetooth printer, it's great – but merely to emphasise that the technology doesn't 'just work' in a plug-and-play way. Some effort/frustration may be required before you can establish a workable PAN (Personal Area Network).

Then again, the same was true of all networking technologies from Ethernet through to the latest crop of wireless 802.11 standards, and indeed of USB and FireWire, too. As so often, a technology developed by geeks but marketed to consumers has to undergo several revisions and user interface overhauls before it finally becomes attractive. In our opinion, Bluetooth isn't there yet.

Keep an eye on developments here:

www.bluetooth.com
www.bluetooth.org

Installing Bluetooth What you need is a Bluetooth adapter of some description, and that depends on what kind of device you want to enable. A USB dongle is perhaps the easiest approach. A laptop can be brought into the PAN with a PC Card adapter (or, again, a USB dongle) and many PDAs accept slot-in adapters. You can also get printer adapters that convert ordinary printers into wireless devices. Our advice is to plan your PAN carefully and buy your Bluetooth kit from one supplier if at all possible. This is the best way to ensure – well, aim towards – pain-free installation.

A Bluetooth mouse and keyboard. Other possibilities include printers, headsets, mobile phones and PDAs.

5

PART **5** # Peripheral devices

A peripheral device is any component in a computer system that isn't actually the computer itself. If you take away the processor, memory and motherboard, all you're left with is a box of bits that falls some way short of a working PC. But the monitor, keyboard, mouse and printer are mere add-ons. So too are the hard disk, CD-ROM and floppy drive. Here we'll look at upgrading the most common external peripherals, beginning with the most important – and expensive – of them all.

Upgrading your monitor

Because monitors are so pricey, manufacturers and retailers of budget – and even high-end – computer systems tend to cut corners here first. But while a 15-inch display unit may have looked just fine in the shop, do you now find yourself shuffling the chair ever closer each day just to see what's going on? Has the picture lost some of its sparkle and colour depth? Have you taken up digital photography or computer gaming and found that your ageing monitor no longer cuts the mustard? It's time to save your eyesight and go for a bigger, better model. Choose wisely and it will serve you well for years – and, unlike the rest of your system, it won't be obsolete as soon as you get it home.

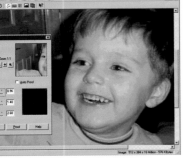

If digital photography is a hobby, you'll need a good monitor to see the results at their best.

What you need to know

There are two main types of computer monitor – CRT (Cathode Ray Tube) and LCD (Liquid Crystal Display). Here's a brief summary of the pros and cons.

Screen size The screen size of a monitor is a diagonal measurement from corner to corner. However, while a 17-inch LCD model will indeed have a viewable screen of 17 inches, as you would hope and expect, the same size of CRT monitor typically offers a *viewable* screen size of only 16 inches or less.

15" LCD = 15" viewable area

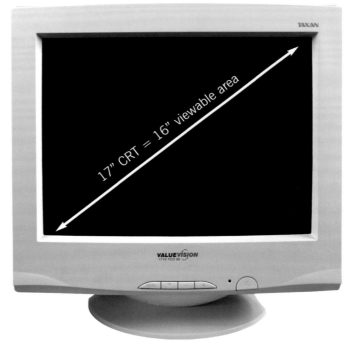

17" CRT = 16" viewable area

This is because the quoted figure is a measure of the cathode ray tube itself, part of which is always hidden from view by the monitor housing. Indeed, we've seen 17-inch monitors that offer just a fraction over 15 inches of visible screen. Look for an 'actual screen area' figure, or whip out a tape measure and make your own comparisons.

Distortion Thanks to clever manufacturing techniques, CRT screens are now much flatter than they once were. This helps to reduce distortion, especially around the edges. Best of the bunch are those imaginatively called 'flat', as opposed to 'flat squared' or 'spherical' (avoid). LCD screens are perfectly flat so distortion issues don't arise.

In fact, there are several different manufacturing techniques and monitor standards. The two terms you are most likely to encounter are shadow mask and aperture grill. The first incorporates a perforated sheet of metal that focuses electron beams on to the screen, often used in FST (Flat Square Tube) models where the curvature of the glass is minimised. The second replaces the perforated sheet with a series of vertical wires through which the beams are channelled. These are held in place by two horizontal wires that can usually be seen (just), if you stare at the screen hard enough. Some people find this irritating but the aperture grill approach means that almost completely flat glass can be used to make a monitor.

Resolution We discussed resolution on p90, where we pointed out that the graphics card and monitor should be matched to produce the best quality picture. However, CRT monitors generally run well and look good at a full range of resolutions whereas LCD screens are optimised to work at a single resolution.

Refresh rate A measure of how many times per second the monitor redraws the image on screen. As a rule, the higher the resolution, the harder it is to maintain a high refresh rate; as another, a high refresh rate means less visible flicker, and that means no headaches or eyestrain. Look for a CRT monitor capable of sustaining a refresh rate of 85Hz at a resolution of 1,024 x 768 and at least 75Hz at 1,280 x 1,024. (Refresh rates are not so important with LCD monitors because of the different display technology: around 60Hz is acceptable.)

TECHIE CORNER

CRT and LCD – the difference!
Trusty old cathode ray tube technology works by firing a beam of electrons at the screen in order to stimulate red, blue and green phosphor dots. By continually drawing lines across the screen, the beam paints a picture across the entire viewable area. Then it does the same thing over and over again many times per second (the refresh rate).

In an LCD monitor, a liquid crystal solution is suspended between two sheets and an electric current switches individual cells (pixels) on and off to block light or let it pass through. In TFT (Thin Film Transistors) models, a tiny transistor controls each pixel. Or, to cut a long story short, CRT works just like your television and LCD just like your digital watch. For full details, look here:
www.pctechguide.com/ 06crtmon.htm
www.pctechguide.com/ 07panels.htm

CRT Screen

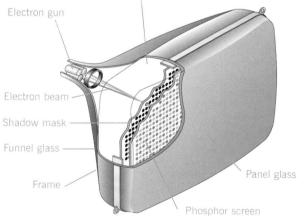

Inner magnetic shield
Electron gun
Electron beam
Shadow mask
Funnel glass
Frame
Panel glass
Phosphor screen

LCD Screen

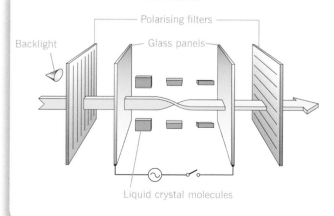

Polarising filters
Backlight
Glass panels
Liquid crystal molecules

Dimensions No comparison here. CRT monitors are big, bulky and heavy; LCDs are neater, much shallower and relatively lightweight. If you're pushed for space or don't fancy bashing a hole in your wall to accommodate the rear end of a CRT monitor, stretch the budget and splash out on LCD. Alternatively, consider 'short neck' CRT monitors where a premium price buys a much reduced tube depth.

Viewing angle CRT screens can be viewed from just about any angle – try it and see – but you need to be sitting pretty straight on to an LCD monitor to see the full picture. Not a big issue, perhaps, and the viewing angles are improving all the time, but LCDs are not ideally suited to communal use. Then again, does your family really sit around the PC on a regular basis?

Analogue or digital? Both CRT and LCD monitors are available with the DVI (Digital Visual Interface) interface, although it's much more common on the latter. We strongly recommend a DVI monitor. You might not notice a dramatic improvement in image quality but at least your monitor will be compatible with your next graphics card or computer.

Price LCD monitors used to be *much* more expensive than CRTs but mass production has brought the prices tumbling down and now they are pretty much standard equipment with new PCs. Also, when you're making comparisons, remember that a 15-inch LCD offers practically the same visible viewing area as the average 17-inch CRT.

There's no getting away from it: LCD monitors are infinitely sleeker and sexier than their CRT cousins.

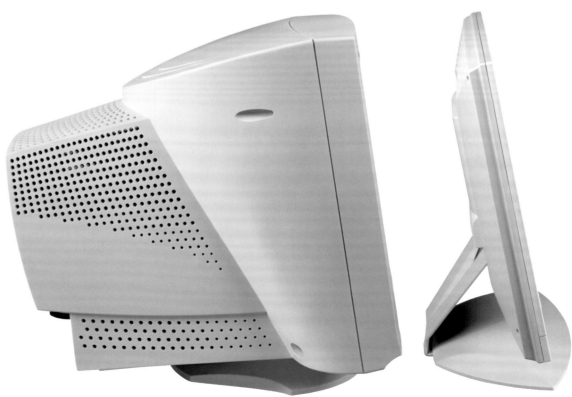

TROUBLE-SHOOTER

No picture? It sounds obvious but make sure that the monitor is plugged in and switched on. **Also check** that the graphics card isn't trying to produce an image at a higher resolution and/or refresh rate than the monitor can handle.

Is the brightness set to zero? It sounds unlikely but it can happen during experimentation with the monitor's own controls. **Failing that**, reconnect your original monitor and see if the picture returns. If so, it's a safe bet that your new monitor is a dud – but do seek out the troubleshooting section in the manual and eliminate all possible problems before sending it back.

Dead pixels It's a fact of life that virtually every TFT LCD monitor sold comes with a dead pixel or two. These look like tiny dots on the screen, and are black or coloured depending on whether a transistor has failed in the off or on position. However, unless your screen is peppered with them to the extent that it detracts from normal use – a rare occurrence indeed – don't worry about it. Besides which, most monitor manufacturers will merely point you to the small print that explains that a few dead pixels are permissible according to the terms of the sale.

Installing your new monitor

On one hand, this is a simple case of switching off your PC, unplugging the old monitor, plugging in the new one, and rebooting. If necessary, use a DVI adapter to connect a digital monitor to an analogue graphics card, or vice versa. Windows then detects that something has changed and launches the New Hardware Found wizard, at which point you'll be prompted to install the monitor's driver. But (you just knew there would be a but), it takes a little more effort to get a perfect picture.

Get tweaking First off, you'll want to experiment with the monitor's own controls. Modern monitors typically have a couple of buttons that control elements of the display, such as brightness, contrast and position (you can adjust the image width and depth to fill the available screen space). Most provide an onscreen display that makes it very much easier to see what you're doing.

As we've seen, the graphics card is responsible for generating the image that appears on screen, and now is the time to tweak its settings to best effect. For instance, you might want to boost the refresh rate to take advantage of your new monitor's increased capabilities. Click Start, point to Settings, click Control Panel, double click Display and open the Settings tab (or right-click the Desktop, select Properties and open Settings from there). Here you can set the resolution (screen area) and colour depth (the maximum number of colours). Click the Advanced button to access further options. Be sure to check and, if necessary, adjust the refresh rate in the Adaptor tab. Set it to the highest rate that your monitor can support at the resolution you've chosen (consult the manual for details). It's generally easier on the eyes to compromise with a lower resolution and a higher refresh rate than the other way around. Remember that LCD monitors are designed to work at one optimum resolution.

Play around with the display settings and any supplied utilities to make the most of your new monitor.

PART

Upgrading your keyboard and mouse

Too many coffee spills made too many sticky keys? Cat got your mouse? Have you outgrown those flimsy, undersized devices so clearly thrown in as an afterthought with your new computer system? Do you want some extra bells and whistles in the shape of shortcut keys and internet buttons on your keyboard and a couple of programmable buttons on your mouse? Or have sore wrists and the onset of RSI (Repetitive Strain Injury) driven you to consider an ergonomic approach?

What you need to know

Very little, in truth, but a few pointers won't go amiss.

Interface Keyboards and mouse both use a small 6-pin PS/2-style plug and socket or, very rarely, a larger 5-pin DIN. Although you can buy adaptors to convert one to the other, it's easier by far to source kit that's immediately compatible with your PC. Alternatively, if you're running Windows 98 or later, consider USB devices. Many USB keyboards have additional sockets that allow you to connect a couple of low-powered devices directly to the keyboard rather than to the back of the computer or to a separate hub. A USB mouse would be the most obvious contender. USB mice are also more responsive and smoother in operation.

Keys and buttons Today's keyboards come with somewhere between 101 and 107 keys as standard. Any reference in the specifications to 'Windows 95' guarantees the inclusion of three

How do 26 letters and 10 digits add up to 100-plus keys?

extra keys that provide quick access to the Start menu and context-sensitive menus (equivalent to a right-click with the mouse in most applications). Some keyboards even have a built-in trackball, which can save a lot of to-ing and fro-ing between the keyboard and the mouse, while many others feature 'hot keys'. These provide shortcuts to programs, instant access to features like speaker volume, and back/forward/stop buttons for browsing the web. In fact, the possibilities are vast. You'll find that some keyboards are designed more for office work and others for playing music and videos. Regardless, you can usually reprogram hot keys to perform the functions that are most useful to you.

Scrolling wheels, programmable buttons, funky colours, with or without wires. What more could you want from a mouse?

Mice can be similarly adept. All have two clickable buttons, some have three, and most now have a central wheel nestling between the left and right buttons. You may find this awkward to use at first but it's a terrific boon for scrolling swiftly through documents and web pages. Indeed, we'd unhesitatingly recommend the wheel as sufficient reason to upgrade an old mouse. Beyond this, you can get mice with additional buttons which can be programmed to do useful things. If your mouse has a thumb-operated button along the side, for instance, you could make this minimise all open windows or click the back button in your browser or do pretty much anything else you like.

Those handy Windows keys are useful shortcuts.

Ergonomics 'Ergonomic' is a marketing term, not a standard and definitely not a science. That said, ergonomic keyboards are designed to maintain a more natural hand and wrist posture, thus helping to prevent symptoms of RSI like carpal tunnel syndrome. The first time you try one, it will feel decidedly odd and distinctly unnatural – but persevere and you'll likely be hooked. Our advice is to seek the testimony of friends and colleagues. Toying with a keyboard for 30 seconds in a shop really doesn't tell you anything.

Do your wrists a favour with an ergonomic design.

This cordless Bluetooth kit includes a base station for easy (ahem) connectivity with other Bluetooth-enabled devices.

Cordless One rather tasty upgrade option is a cordless keyboard and mouse. Most cordless devices use RF (Radio Frequency) technology whereby every press of a key or click of a button transmits a signal to a small receiver connected to the PC. More recently, Bluetooth-enabled keyboards and mice have been widely marketed. In either case, the end result is a neater desk. Cordless devices are also ideal if you have a computer connected to your TV and you want to control the onscreen action from a distance.

Optical mice This style of modern mouse has a light sensor on its underbelly that detects motion and relays this to the computer. No more de-fluffing.

Trackballs Instead of sliding a mouse around a mat, a trackball stays stationary while you move the screen cursor by manipulating a big ball, just like the arcade games of yore. Some people love them; others wouldn't give them desk-room.

Optical mice run fluff-free for ever.

A trackball is a motionless mouse.

TECHIE CORNER

Under the (key) covers
There are two main manufacturing methods for keyboards. Switch-based devices have micro-switches under every key and click satisfyingly with every key press. Capacitive keyboards incorporate a single sensitive membrane beneath the keys. Every tap makes an electronic connection that sends a signal to the computer via a microprocessor. No clicks here – the keys generally have a smooth, quiet action – but capacitive keyboards tend to last longer because there are fewer bits to break. Then again, unlike switch-based keyboards, they cannot usually be repaired if they go wrong. Such is life.

Tablets As an alternative to the mouse, or even as an add-on, consider a graphics tablet. With these, you draw and tap on a flat tablet with a cordless pen in order to mimic the actions of a mouse. Tablets are designed primarily for use with drawing and photo-editing applications but can also be a most natural – and accurate – way to control the onscreen cursor.

You can use a pen and tablet instead of dragging a mouse around a mat.

TROUBLE-SHOOTER

You're very unlikely to run into difficulties installing a keyboard. However, one possibility, albeit rare, is that you plug in a new USB keyboard, reboot, and find that you can't enter your user name or password (assuming you have password protection set up). The problem is that the USB device's driver has not yet been installed, so Windows doesn't know that the keyboard exists and thus cannot recognise its commands. The workaround is to switch the PC off once more, plug in your old keyboard while leaving the USB keyboard connected and enter your user name and password on the old device. When Windows starts, the drivers for the USB keyboard can be installed. Next time you shut down the PC,

unplug the old keyboard. You should now have no further problems. Alternatively, try clicking Cancel with the mouse (make it a PS/2 model to avoid the same difficulty!) when the password prompt appears. This should bypass the security feature and enable the driver to be installed.

Installing a new keyboard and mouse

What can we say? If you're replacing one PS/2 device with another, turn off your computer, unplug the old, and plug in the new. The only thing you really need to watch is that you plug the mouse cable into the mouse socket, usually colour-coded green, and the keyboard cable into the keyboard socket, usually colour-coded purple.

If you're adding a USB device, do just the same but connect the new hardware to any free USB port on the computer or, if you have one, a USB hub. Windows will then recognise the addition and ask you to install the driver software. Pop the supplied CD-ROM in the drive and follow directions.

Thereafter, you can activate fancy features and program extra keys and buttons with the supplied software utility. Failing this, open the mouse and keyboard configuration tools in Windows. Click Start > Settings > Control Panel and then Mouse or Keyboard. In Windows XP, the route is Start > Control Panel > Printers and Other Hardware.

Colour coding makes a simple job foolproof.

PART  Upgrading your speakers

Decent speakers can make even the crummiest sound card sound better than it deserves to, but a top-notch sound card is wasted on those tiny, tinny units usually bundled 'free' with computers. So, be you music lover or musician, computer games player or DVD movie fan, invest in a decent set of bins if you want to rock the house.

What you need to know

Hi-fi buffs will have little trouble with speaker specifications but the rest of us need a little help.

Subwoofers and satellites A subwoofer is a big-speaker-in-a-box that sits on the floor and boosts the bass signal. Satellites are smaller but still full-range speakers positioned left and right of the listener in order to produce a stereo effect. Such a setup is described as 2.1 (two satellites plus a subwoofer), 4.1 (four satellites plus a subwoofer), or 5.1, or 7.1, or whatever.

Surround sound This is the effect created when a second set of speakers is positioned behind the listener, one to each side, to complement a pair of stereo speakers positioned left and right of the sound source. A separate subwoofer handles the bass tones and, in a 5.1 setup, a further satellite is positioned directly in front of the listener. A sound card capable of surround sound then pumps different elements of the multi-channel audio signal to different speakers. The enveloping effect can be quite spooky.

Stereo speakers are fine for listening to music but you might want to invest in a 5.1 sound system if you plan to watch DVD movies on your PC. This setup goes further still in the surround sound stakes with no fewer than seven satellite speakers.

Digital input Most sound cards output an analogue signal – they have to convert the computer's native digital signal to analogue in the process, which is daft – but some have digital outputs, usually labelled SPDIF (Sony/Philips Digital Interface). If yours is thus equipped, it's worthwhile getting digital speakers to complement it.

TECHIE CORNER

Going overboard
Computer audio technology, both analogue and digital, continues to evolve apace. We haven't even touched on the scientific stuff, such as signal to noise ratios and frequency responses. The bottom line is this: if you really want to use your PC as a sound system, you are truly spoilt for choice and should research the multitude of options carefully; but if you just want a decent sound quality for playing CDs and the odd game, a mid-range, mid-price multi-channel sound card and a decent set of 4.1 or 5.1 surround sound speakers will blow your socks off. To find out much, much more, go here:
http://www.dolby.com

You can expand your options with a digital decoder. However, this is overkill for a straightforward PC system.

Satellite speakers usually connect to the back end of the subwoofer.

Separate decoder Some speaker systems are available with a separate standalone decoder. Such a unit usually has multiple inputs and is most useful in a home entertainment environment where you want to connect, say, a DVD player, TV, hi-fi, portable music player and PC to the same set of speakers. A decoder can also accept a raw, encoded audio signal from a computer's DVD drive (or from a basic DVD player, come to that) and decode it into the multi-channel signals required to drive a surround sound setup.

USB Sound cards normally convert the digital signal from audio CDs and MP3 files into an analogue signal, and pipe it to the speakers. As we've mentioned, digital sound cards skip this conversion and broadcast a 'cleaner' digital signal. However, it's also possible to buy digital speakers that connect to the PC through the USB port, thereby bypassing the sound card altogether. You have to be pretty committed to aural fidelity to spot the difference, and they're not the easiest things to configure, but we thought we ought to mention them. Incidentally, USB speakers will only work with audio CDs if your CD/DVD drives supports Digital Audio Extraction, see p82.

Spaghetti This is what you get when you install a 4.1, 5.1 or 7.1 speaker system. Be prepared to trip over more wiring than you thought possible and be sure to follow the setup directions carefully.

Installing your new speakers

Plug them in to the audio out channel(s) on your sound card, connect the power supply to a wall socket, and switch them on. Sounds too simple to be true? Well, yes and no. No, because hooking up stereo speakers to your PC really is as straightforward as that. The main thing to watch is where the PC has two sets of speaker sockets: one set nestled in the motherboard's input/output panel (the same panel that holds the mouse and keyboard sockets) and another on an expansion card. In such cases, the computer has integrated audio and a separate sound card: see p17 for an example. The sound card is always the one to go with here.

But yes, connecting speakers can also be absurdly complicated when surround sound is involved. You'll first have to run cables from the sound card to the sub-woofer, possibly via an external decoder, and from there make all the satellite speaker connections. This is definitely a job to be undertaken with the speaker supplier's manual in hand.

High-tech speakers need to be positioned correctly and configured with software.

PART 5 Upgrading your printer

Inkjet printers have long been bundled 'free' with new computer systems. Unbelievable value, screamed the ads, but the reality was unbelievably duff print quality. If you ran your business cards off on one of those ... well, colleagues would accept them politely but mark you down as a cheapskate amateur.

How times have changed. Even the cheapest inkjet on the market today, bundled or otherwise, is a remarkably adept device. But there's a sting in the tail, as we shall see.

Prints charming More on the detailed specs in a second but do take a moment to consider why you need a printer and what you want it to do for you. The first decision is choosing between an inkjet and a laser. If crisp, clear text is paramount, particularly for business, then a laser printer is a must. But if you'd like some colour in your life, an inkjet is the obvious solution. Or at least it was until recently. Colour laser printers have plummeted in price and you may now find a model that justifies a little additional outlay. However, colour lasers are still much better suited to printing colour documents than to colour printing per se, particularly when it comes to photographs. This may change, but for now we'd recommend a colour laser for spicier business stationery but a good inkjet is still essential if you want to print digital images at a high resolution (i.e. top quality).

A modern inkjet printer can produce stunning colours at a high resolution.

Some printers are geared up to print on a wide variety of media – envelopes, various paper sizes and weights, transparencies, address stickers, labels for your home-burned CDs and so forth – while others are pretty much A4 and US letter size or nothing. Some run on batteries for under-the-arm instant portability; others can print direct from a digital camera without a computer in sight. There really is a printer out there for every purpose and the prices just keep on falling.

What you need to know

It pays to research the market carefully and we'd recommend reading a few comparative group tests in computer magazines to see what's currently hot and what's not. Such is the pace of evolution that last month's super-duper photo-realistic miracle of modern engineering is invariably this month's overpriced smudger. Here's a guide to the main considerations.

Interface There are now four connection choices: traditional parallel port; newer USB, at either speed, for faster data processing; newer-still Bluetooth for wireless connectivity; and a network interface for sharing a printer with multiple computers. For 'normal' use, a fast USB 2 interface is now the default standard.

From portable to professional, there are printers to suit every output.

Go for a USB printer if your PC supports it.

Consumables Inkjet printers use ink supplied in replaceable cartridges, and inkjets use powdered toner. As a rule, colour inkjet printers are cheaper to buy than monochrome laser printers but more expensive to run. Irritatingly, the cheapest printers often use the most expensive cartridges – and therein lies the sting in the tail. Do the sums: a giveaway inkjet that costs more than its own purchase price to refill each time is not much of a bargain.

You think we're joking? Far from it. There are £29 printers out there that cost considerably more to replenish with fresh ink. The long-term running costs can also be staggering: one recent study found that a £40 printer could cost nearly £1,800 to run over 18 months.

Be aware that if you're tempted to refill old cartridges with cheap ink – and there are plenty of companies who'll happily sell you a kit to do just that – you can save a pretty penny but you'll almost certainly invalidate the printer's warranty. You'll also get in a mess. By all means try out your local high street refill company

Insist on an inkjet printer that uses separate black and coloured ink cartridges.

TECHIE CORNER

Print technologies
The two grand impact printers of yesteryear were clattering, clumsy affairs. Dot-matrix models struck pins against an ink-impregnated ribbon – the greater the number of pins, the better the quality of the letters – while daisy-wheel machines hammered protruding characters on a rotating disk. Neither type could print pictures

and both are now all but obsolete, certainly on the domestic desktop (which is not to say that you won't find them bashing out despatch notes in warehouses around the world: if staff have to shout, there's an impact printer at work).

Laser printers use light to generate a charged image on a drum and heat-fuse powdery black toner on to paper. Inkjet printers

squirt tiny globules of ink straight at the page. This used to mean that pages came out all sopping wet and soggy, but no longer. It's all so much more refined these days, and a good deal more flexible. Even the cheapest inkjet printer suffices for homework projects and printing out web pages, and the humblest laser can produce professional quality text.

High-quality paper is a worthwhile investment for photographic reproduction.

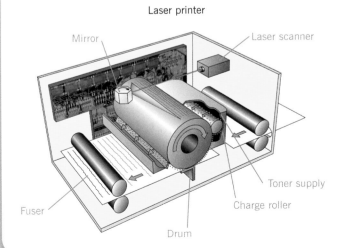

Laser printer

Mirror

Laser scanner

Fuser

Toner supply

Charge roller

Drum

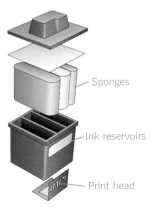

Inkjet cartridge

Sponges

Ink reservoirs

Print head

and see if you're happy with the resulting quality. An alternative is buying 'compatible' cartridges that install in your printer just like manufacturer-branded originals but cost considerably less.

Be sure to choose a printer that uses separate black and colour ink cartridges, as there's nothing more wasteful than throwing out perfectly good colours just because the black runs out (and vice versa).

Resolution This is a rating of the level of detail in a printed image, measured in terms of dots per inch. Look for at least 600dpi or 1,200dpi. Beware references to 'enhanced' or 'interpolated' resolution, as this involves software sophistry and is not a true reflection of a device's ability. Also check that a quoted resolution of 600dpi means 600 x 600 (i.e. 600 dots per inch horizontally and vertically). Sometimes, 600 x 300 resolutions are misleadingly described as 600dpi.

Memory Laser printers have to buffer data from the PC as they work and so incorporate RAM chips. The bare minimum is 512KB but 2 or 4MB makes for faster, more reliable performance. Many models' memory can be upgraded, which could be helpful if your work rate shoots up or you print a lot of graphics.

Speed Most manufacturers claim that their printers are capable of churning out X pages of Y-sized paper with Z% ink coverage per minute. That would be just fine if they all used the same criteria, but they don't. Sadly, it's up to you to get out the calculator and do the maths. However, do you really care how

If your laser printer is slowing you down, see if you can upgrade its memory.

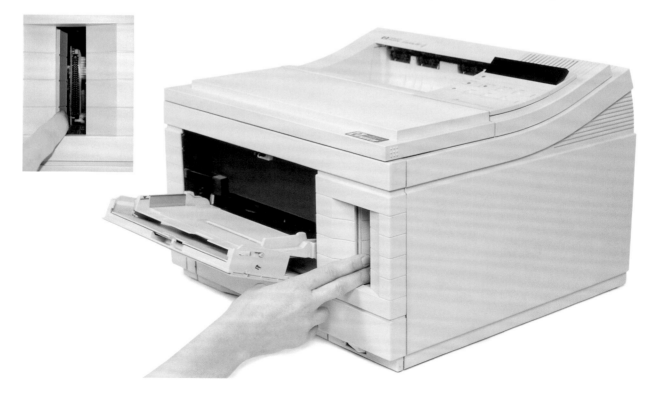

fast your printer is? Most domestic tasks are hardly 'mission critical' so we'd suggest concentrating more on quality than on speed.

Media Virtually all laser printers work just fine with cheap, plain paper (so-called laser paper is just a little whiter and brighter). However, it is worth investing in specialist papers to get the best results from an inkjet. Don't feel that you necessarily have to buy same-brand, though; a little experimentation with alternative papers often pays dividends.

Duty cycle This is the manufacturer's measure of a printer's maximum workload. A monthly duty cycle of, say, 12,000 pages means just that: don't print any more than 12,000 pages in any given month if you want the device to continue performing at its peak. Clearly, this has much more relevance in an office setting than at home.

Lifespan How long is a piece of string? Keep refilling an inkjet printer when it runs dry and it should last 'forever' – or at least until you upgrade your operating system and discover that it no longer supports your now-obsolete device! The photosensitive drum in a laser printer must be periodically replaced, usually at quite some cost. Look for a drum lifespan of somewhere between 15,000 and 30,000 pages, and be sure to factor this in when making price comparisons. Sometimes, the toner cartridge and drum are combined in a single unit.

Software You may find a whole heap of application software in the box. Inkjets typically come with a photo editing package and something along the lines of a make-your-own-greetings-cards utility. But don't be swayed by the software alone: it's not nearly as important as the hardware specifications.

Printers, particularly inkjets, often come with a full range of applications.

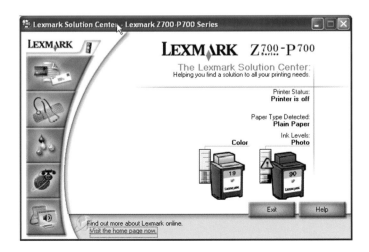

Installing a new printer

All printers have a pre-installation routine that generally involves removing strategic strips of packing tape, loading the ink cartridges or toner, bolting on feeder and output trays, and perhaps running a self-test procedure. Follow the manual's instructions to the letter.

Thereafter, the routine depends upon whether it's a parallel or USB model. In the latter case, Windows will detect the device as soon as it's plugged into a USB port and ask for the installation CD-ROM. However, some printer manufacturers insist that you load driver software before connecting the printer. Again, read the manual carefully.

If you have a printer that connects via the parallel port, you must manually inform Windows of its presence. In Windows 98 and Millennium Edition, follow these steps:

 Start

 Settings

 Control Panel

 Printers

Connect your printer to the parallel port with its cable and turn it on.

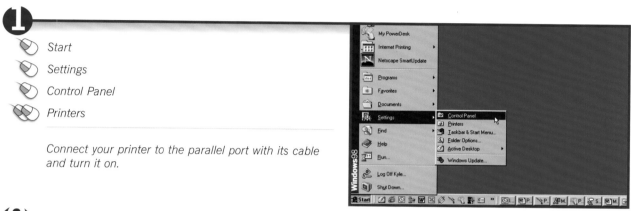

 Add printer

 Your printer

 Next

If you don't have an installation CD-ROM for your printer – perhaps you picked it up second hand – you can ask Windows to install a default driver from its own database. Unless your model is ultra-obscure, you should find it here. Select it from the list and proceed.

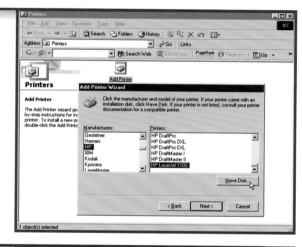

 Have Disk

 OK

Ordinarily, though, the Have Disk route is the one to take. Insert the installation CD-ROM in its drive, click the Have Disk button and tell Windows which drive to look in. You will probably be prompted to restart the PC at the end of the process.

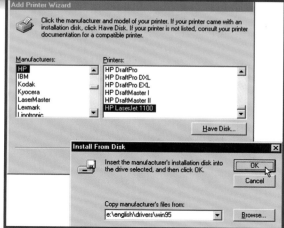

Finally, install any application programs supplied with the device. The manual may suggest that you run a print alignment utility before you start printing. Don't skip this step as it determines the accuracy of your prints.

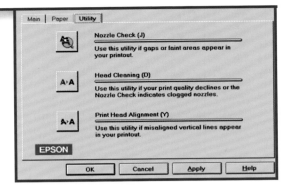

The Windows XP routine

In Windows XP, the procedure is much the same but there's a handy Add Printer wizard on hand to step you through. As it says at the outset: 'If you have a Plug and Play printer that connects through a USB port… you do not need this wizard.' That's the beauty of USB: plug in a device and Windows either works with it immediately (if the drivers have been installed previously) or prompts to install the drivers first time around. With the old parallel interface, none of this is possible. However, the wizard makes reasonably light work of installation.

TROUBLE-SHOOTER

If print quality isn't up to scratch, look for and run a diagnostic program. This should be included on the installation CD-ROM. Inkjet print heads benefit from periodic cleaning but this is a process controlled by software (i.e. don't take a cotton bud to an ink cartridge).

Most printers also let you perform a rudimentary self-test just by pushing a button or two on the device itself. Consult the manual.

Does Windows know that this is the default printer i.e. the one that all applications should use without asking? Return to the Printers folder (Step 1 p129) and look for a big bold tick next to the appropriate icon. If it's not there, right-click the icon and select Set as Default.

Printer drivers are usually updated on a regular basis so it makes sense to visit the

manufacturer's website periodically. A new driver can often resolve bugs and glitches and may add some smart new features.

Unfortunately, printers have many moving parts and the software that turns a computer-generated digital document into a printed page is complex. In other words, lots can go wrong. The upside is that virtually all problems are easily rectified. Again, check the manual for guidance and consult the manufacturer's website.

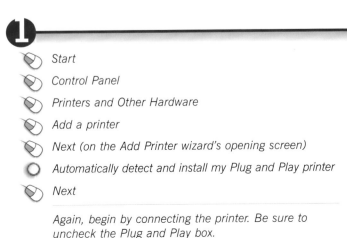

○ *Start*

○ *Control Panel*

○ *Printers and Other Hardware*

○ *Add a printer*

○ *Next (on the Add Printer wizard's opening screen)*

○ *Automatically detect and install my Plug and Play printer*

○ *Next*

Again, begin by connecting the printer. Be sure to uncheck the Plug and Play box.

Use the following port: LPT1

 Next

For obscure reasons, Windows knows the parallel port as LPT1. Since that's where your printer is connected, select it from the list. It should, in fact, be pre-selected for you by default.

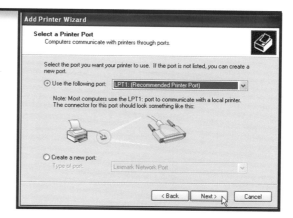

 Your printer

 Have Disk

You can either select your printer from the list and click Next, in which case Windows will install a driver from its own database; or click Have Disk and use the installation CD-ROM that came with the printer. The latter is better, for the driver is likely to be more up to date (i.e. less buggy). Either way, this will get the printer working.

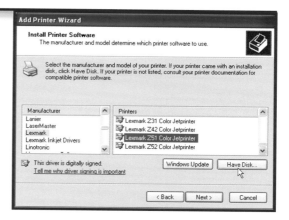

 Printer name

 Yes

 Next

Finally, give your printer a name or accept the proffered suggestion and decide whether or not you want it to be the default printer. The default printer is the one that all applications will use without question. If you only have one printer, of course, it will be the default device by, er, default.

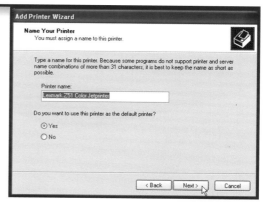

PART  Upgrading your scanner

A scanner takes a picture of a piece of paper and turns it into a digital image file that you can view and edit on your computer. There, it's as simple as that. So what might you use one for?

Well, you could scan a paper document into your PC and then fax it through the modem. Or you could print out a hard copy or two and thus emulate a photocopier. You might scan recipes, magazine articles, newspaper clippings or handwritten notes and preserve them forever on your hard disk, or perhaps email them to friends as file attachments. You could scan your snapshots, remove the red-eye and embarrassing ex-partners with an image editing program, and publish them on your website or in a newsletter. You might even scan every shred of paper in your possession and index and archive it all neatly on disc, so creating a truly paperless home/office. The uses for a scanner are indeed many and varied.

   Like printers, 'free' scanners are often bundled with new computers to add the illusion of value but invariably they're second rate models. Plus any scanner more than a couple of years old is going to be vastly outclassed by today's generation.

Flatbed is the most common design for scanners. However, there are plenty of alternatives, including truly portable pen-sized models.

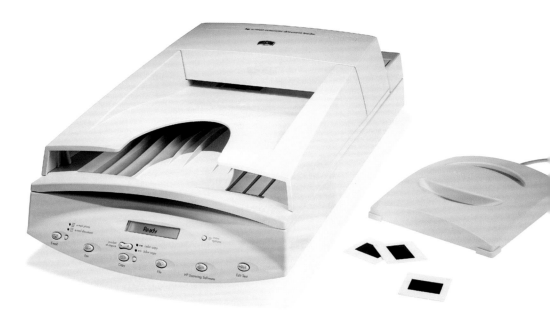

What you need to know

The language of scanner technology is unfamiliar to most but in fact there's nothing too complicated.

An ADF attachment saves time and effort when making multiple scans.

Design Scanners come in all shapes and sizes but flatbed models are by far the most popular. These look just like mini photocopiers: you lift the lid, place a document face down on the glass plate, close the lid and initiate the scan using software on your PC. Any flatbed should handle an A4 page with room to spare, and the lids are often cleverly hinged or completely removable in order that bulky objects like books also can be scanned.

Alternative designs include handheld scanners that you manually sweep across the page and sheetfeed models where you feed pages through a roller mechanism one at a time.

Interface SCSI was once common but usually meant having to install an adaptor on an internal expansion card, which was fiddly and expensive. USB is now the interface of choice but the slower parallel port also suffices.

Resolution The detail of a scanned image is measured in terms of dots per inch. More is better. Look for at least 600 x 1,200dpi true, or optical, resolution (as opposed to interpolated resolution – usually a much higher figure but not a true reflection of a scanner's capability).

Colour depth This describes how many colours a scanner can distinguish. Older scanners stuck at 24 bits, which equates to recognising nearly 17 million colours, but new models scan at 36 bits and are moving to 42 or even 48 bits. The greater colour depths help scanners to deal with bright and dark images as well as distinguish finer colour nuances. For scanning magazines and photos at home, a 30-bit scanner is more than adequate.

TWAIN In order for scanners to communicate with a wide range of software applications, they virtually all support a common standard called TWAIN (Technology Without An Interesting Name, according to urban legend). This means that even a word

processor or spreadsheet program can import an image straight from a scanner.

An adapter lets you scan film transparencies and slides as easily as printed pages.

ADF Strictly an optional extra, Automatic Document Feeders feed documents through a flatbed scanner one page at a time. Very useful for high volume work.

Transparency adaptor This is a bolt-on accessory with a built-in light that enables a scanner to scan photographic transparencies.

OCR If you scanned the page that you're reading right now into your computer, you might think that you could immediately cut, copy and paste the text. But you'd be wrong. A scanned page is merely an image that makes no distinction between words and pictures. OCR, or Optical Character Recognition, is the process of turning a scanned image into editable text. Essentially, software 'reads' the image and determines which bits are words (and, crucially, which words) and which bits are design elements and pictures. OCR is almost never 100% successful but the best programs let you proof read as you go along to correct mistakes. Most scanners come with at least a 'lite' OCR package in the box.

Speed As with printers, some scanners are marginally quicker than others. The interface makes the biggest difference: SCSI scanners are quick but rare; parallel scanners should be avoided; USB 1.1 scanners are ideal; but USB 2 (Hi-Speed USB) scanners are best of all.

Software Look for at least a basic image manipulation program with your new toy. After all, you're going to want to tweak all those scanned images. For real ease of use, some scanners have a one-touch button that fires them into action without fussing with software. Others start working as soon as you open or close the lid. However, in most cases you'll run a TWAIN-compliant application on your PC and control the scanning process from there.

Installing your new scanner
You install a USB scanner in exactly the same way as any other USB peripheral: connect it to a free USB port on your PC and install the driver from the supplied CD-ROM when prompted.

Scanners come in parallel and SCSI flavours but USB is a good compromise between speed and convenience.

PART ⑤ Multi-function devices

As you'll no doubt have noticed during a previous excursion to any computer shop, there is an alternative to buying a separate printer and scanner. We're talking, of course, about multi-function devices, or MFDs. An MFD neatly combines print and scan functions in a single box.

One of the immediate advantages is that most MFDs also work like photocopiers: lift the scanner lid, place your document face-down on the glass plate, press the Copy button, and out pops a (scanned and printed) hard copy.

What's more, many MFDs also have built-in modems, which means they can both send and receive faxes. If you remember what we said earlier, a modem can handle faxes just as easily as an internet connection. A fax-capable MFD simply takes advantage of this. In fact, faxing with an MFD is usually a much simpler process than fiddling with modem software on the screen: the scanner takes a photo of your document, you type in a telephone number, and the modem sends the document through the phone line to any fax machine on the planet.

An MFD can be a printer (inkjet or laser), a scanner, a photocopier and a fax machine. They cost less – much less, in fact – than the combined cost of separate devices and they offer tremendous convenience, not least because they require only one plug and one cable connection to your PC. So is there a downside?

Well, the printer component in any MFD is by far the most important and it used to be true that MFDs tended to offer inferior print quality when compared with dedicated printers. But that's no longer the case. We'd merely advise that you check the specs carefully and judge an MFD just as you'd judge a standalone printer. The only real trouble with a decent MFD is the risk that a minor hardware failure in just one element could see the whole shebang shipped off for repair, leaving you sans printer, scanner, copier and fax. Still, balance that with the convenience and cost advantage and you may well feel that an MFD is too good to resist.

A fax-capable MFD may be the only office peripheral you need.

PART **6** # Home networking

Although you can prolong the useful lifespan of a computer almost indefinitely with well-chosen upgrades, there may come a time when you just can't resist starting afresh with a brand-new system. Or perhaps you buy a new PC for the kids, or invest in a laptop. Whatever the reasons, it is becoming increasingly common to find two or more computers in the household – at which point, when you tire of running between them transferring files on floppy disks, it makes practical sense to link them together.

PART

The basics of home networking

The benefits of networking are manifest and significant. Any computer on the network can access files stored on any other computer's hard disk; they can share a single printer regardless of which computer it happens to be connected to; and, most important of all, they can share a single connection to the internet. This means that you can have two or more computers online together without having to invest in additional phone lines.

What you need to know

Speed The most common connection standard used in home networking – or Local Area Networking (LAN) – is Ethernet. This is generally available in three speeds:

● 10Base-T (Ethernet) Data is transferred at a maximum rate of 10 megabits per second

● 100Base-T (Fast Ethernet) Data is transferred at a maximum rate of 100 megabits per second

● 1000Base-T (Gigabit Ethernet) Data is transferred at a maximum rate of 1,000 megabits per second

For home use, 10Base-T is ample, 100Base-T desirable and 1000Base-T overkill.

A couple of Network Interface Cards plus a cable equals one home network.

Interface Many modern PCs are now network-ready but Ethernet can easily be added by means of a Network Interface Card (NIC). Most cards are sold as '10/100', which means they can run at either Ethernet or Fast Ethernet speeds. NICs always use the PCI interface.

Wiring Ethernet cables come in two main flavours: coaxial and twisted pair. Some NICs have connectors for both but the most common option for home use is a twisted pair cable with RJ-45 connectors on either end. An RJ-45 connector looks like a larger version of the RJ-11 connector on your modem cable or telephone. Always buy 'Category 5' cables because they support all speeds of Ethernet and can be reused if you ever upgrade a network from 10Base-T to 100Base-T or 1000Base-T.

Hubs and switches A hub is a box that sits between networked computers to facilitate the free flow of data. Hubs are generally pretty dumb and play no active part in managing data flow, but some incorporate switches that 'intelligently' control the traffic. A switch can avoid networking bottle-necks but it's certainly not essential for a small home network.

Topology Local Area Networks can be set up in many ways. By far the simplest is a peer-to-peer arrangement, in which each PC is an equal partner on the network. The alternative is a client-server model where one computer – the server – controls all the action. This is definitely overkill and over-complicated for home use.

Software As we shall see, it is easy to set up home networking without using any extra software if your PC runs Windows Millennium Edition (Me). Windows 98 Second Edition introduced Internet Connection Sharing, which was a big step forward from Windows 95's limited networking capabilities, but the Home Networking Wizard in Me is a pretty compelling reason to upgrade from 98 if you're serious about networking. The latest version of Windows, XP, makes networking a complete cakewalk. However, its system requirements are too high for many older systems, so we'll assume here that you have Me on board.

An RJ-45 Ethernet cable.

A peer-to-peer network is perfect for hooking together two PCs but a hub adds expansion possibilities.

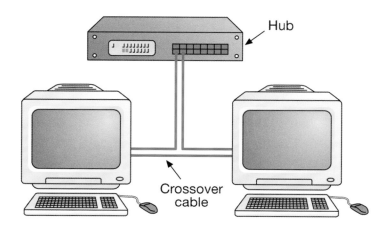

Hub

Crossover cable

PART # A simple crossover cable network

You can connect any two PCs quickly and easily with a couple of Network Interface Cards and a single cable. This is what we'll look at first.

1

Keep things simple by buying a pair of identical 10Base-T or 100Base-T cards with RJ-45 ports. You'll also need a Category 5 crossover cable. This is not a standard Ethernet cable but rather one in which the wiring has been specially manipulated to enable the two-way flow of data without the need for a hub. Ask for help if you're in any doubt.

2

Install one Network Interface Card in the first computer. The method is identical to adding any PCI expansion card (see, for example, the step-by-step USB card upgrade on p.109). Follow the card manufacturer's instructions and install the driver software when prompted.

3

Data passes through a network according to a strict set of rules, or protocol, and the software that comes with your NIC should ensure that all necessary components are installed. Click Start, Settings, Control Panel and double-click the Network icon. In the Configuration tab, you should see entries for at least one of these protocols: NetBEUI, IPX/SPX or TCP/IP.

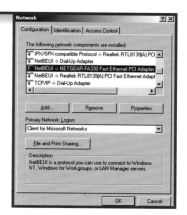

4

Also ensure that Client for Microsoft Networks is the selected entry from the Primary Network Logon drop-down list. If it is not there, click the Add button, highlight Client in the next window, click Add, select Client for Microsoft Networks, and click Add once again. Have your Windows installation CD to hand in case you are prompted for it.

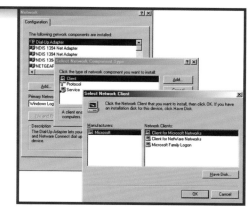

5

Still in the Configuration area of the Network dialogue box, click the File and Print Sharing button and place a tick in both boxes. This ensures that you will be able to access files and print documents across the network.

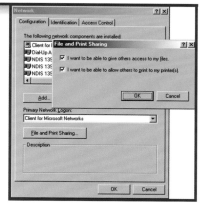

6

Finally, look in the Identification tab and give your computer a meaningful name and, optionally, description. Type MSHOME in the Workgroup field. Close the Network dialogue and restart when prompted. Now install the second NIC in the second PC, repeat each of these steps, and connect the two computers by plugging the crossover cable into the NICs.

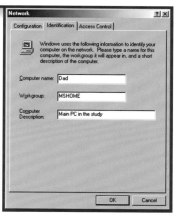

PART  Home Networking Wizard

To get your fledgling network up and running, you need to tell each computer a little about how it is expected to behave. In Windows Millennium Edition, double click the My Network Places icon on the Desktop, run the Home Networking Wizard and follow the prompts. In Windows XP, double click My Network Places and use the Set up a home or small office network shortcut. You can also access network settings and wizards from the Control Panel. It's pretty much plain sailing but here are the important points to note:

Start with the PC that you usually use for internet access or, if one of the PCs is running Windows XP but the other isn't, start on the XP machine. When the Internet Connection dialogue box appears, check the 'direct connection to my ISP' option. Later, when you run the wizard on the second PC, check the 'connection to another computer on my home network' option instead. This sets up Internet Connection Sharing.

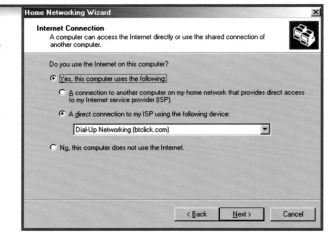

The wizard will ask you for the name of your workgroup and recommend that you accept the default suggestion of MSHOME. This is just fine: the important point is that all computers on a network must use the same workgroup name. You can also rename your computer at this point if you wish.

Now you will be asked if you want to share folders and printers. Accept the recommendation to share the My Documents folder and place a tick against any printers currently connected.

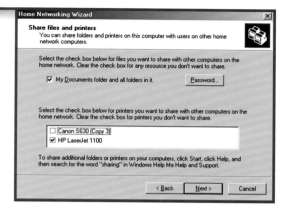

Finally, the wizard will ask if you wish to make a Home Networking Setup disk. This makes it easier to configure other computers in your network and is important if you are currently on a Windows XP machine and need to network a non-XP PC. However, it's not worthwhile if both computers have the same version of Windows. Instead, simply run the wizard on the second PC now. Restart both computers when prompted.

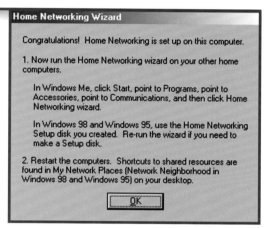

Sharing

In Windows Me, double click the My Network Places icon, double click Entire Network, and finally double click MSHOME or whatever name you gave to your workgroup. You should now be able to 'see' the other networked computer. Double click its icon and have a look in its My Documents folder. Try dragging and dropping files from one PC to the other. That's the wonder of networking!

It's easy to extend or restrict file and folder sharing in a network. For instance, you might wish to provide unrestricted access to one computer's entire hard disk. Double click My Computer, right-click the hard disk icon (C: drive), select Sharing, and then check the Shared As option. Every file and folder on this disk can now be seen, copied, modified and – importantly – deleted by someone using the other networked PC.

Hence the importance of password protection: with drive and folder sharing, you have the opportunity to control the limits of network access. Read-Only access, for instance, means that someone who knows your password can use your files but not delete or modify them.

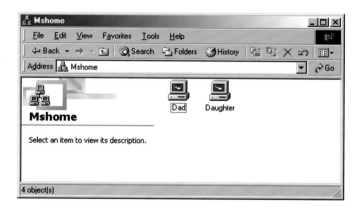

Networked computers in the same workgroup can share files and an internet connection.

Windows XP's Shared Documents folder is the natural home for shared files and folders.

Windows XP Home Edition employs a rather simpler method of file sharing called, of course, Simple File Sharing. The idea here is that any file, folder or drive is either shared or not shared, and is shared or not shared equally with every user on the network. Passwords don't play a part. The safeguard is that when you share anything, you can choose whether or not to allow network users to change your files. Leaving this option unchecked is equivalent to granting read-only access i.e. people can see (and copy) your files, but not change or delete the originals.

XP Professional can work in just the same way but also includes advanced options to grant access permission on a user-by-user basis. It's enough to make you head spin, which is why the best spun heads always end up as IT managers and systems administrators.

Every Windows XP PC also has a folder called Shared Documents that is shared automatically whenever the computer joins a network. This is the easiest and safest way to share files and folders: if you want to share something, copy or move it to Shared Documents; and if you don't, don't.

Take care when you share. Leave this box unchecked when you share a folder to prevent other people from changing – or potentially deleting – your files.

Use passwords to protect your files.

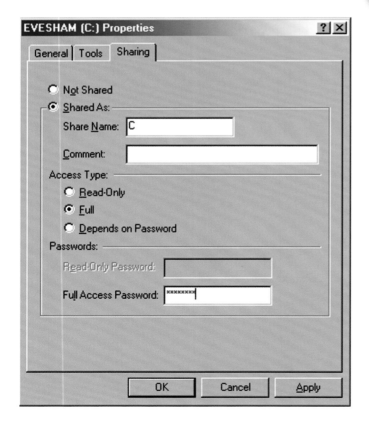

TROUBLE-SHOOTER

Although a simple peer-to-peer network should 'just work', there will be times when one computer doesn't 'see' the others. In our experience, the most common cause is a loose cable. Failing that, restart one, both or all the PCs to reconnect the network. You can also run the Home Networking Wizard at any time to check each computer's settings.

If you have problems with shared internet access in Windows Millennium Edition, try running the Internet Connection Wizard (click Start > Programs > Accessories > Communications > Internet Connection Wizard) on the networked PC that doesn't connect directly to the internet. Select 'I want to connect through a local area network' and then tick the 'Automatic discovery of proxy server' option.

Windows 98 users don't have

the advantage of the Home Networking Wizard but it's still possible to get your computers connected. Look here for help from Microsoft:
http://support.microsoft.com/ default.aspx?kbid=814235& product=w98

Beyond the basics, networking is a big, complex subject. Here are some excellent web links for further information and advice:
www.homepcnetwork.com
www.practicallynetworked.com
w ww.howstuffworks.com/ home-network.htm
www.microsoft.com/homenet

PART 6   Taking it further

The advantages of a crossover cable connection as described above are that it's simple to set up and requires little in the way of hardware. However, there is one serious limitation: there is no way to hook up any further PCs. In other words, your network has no scope for expansion. So...

Hub networking made simple with a kit.

Kitting up

The good news is that you set up a hub-based network in just the same way as a crossover connection. The only real difference is that you use standard (i.e. non-crossover) Ethernet cables and connect each PC to the hub rather than directly to each other. It's possible to buy complete network-in-a-box kits that include a couple of NICs, a hub or switch and all the cables you need. Some also come with software that gets everything up and running first time more easily than the Home Networking Wizard. Be sure to check the speed rating on the hub and cards – 10Base-T or 100Base-T – and note the number of available ports on the hub (you need one for every PC on the network).

Going wireless

As if you didn't have enough computer wiring to trip over already, home networking generally requires you to run cables from room to room in order to connect your computers. However, if you're feeling flush, consider the wireless alternative. Today's most prolific technology is known as 802.11, or Wi-Fi. This a particularly attractive option for laptop owners since you can tap into the full resources of your network at will without fussing with cables: all you need is a removable PC card in the laptop and a wireless access point connected to the network hub. The range for wireless networking varies but you can expect to maintain a fast, unbroken connection around your home, walls and ceilings notwithstanding.

There are three versions of Wi-Fi around right now:

- IEEE 802.11b Data is transferred at a maximum rate of 11 megabits per second
- IEEE 802.11a Data is transferred at a maximum rate of 54 megabits per second
- IEEE 802.11g Data is transferred at a maximum rate of 54 megabits per second

Of these, 802.11b has long been the norm but the faster 802.11g – which is backwards-compatible with 802.11b, so older hardware will still work on an 802.11g network – is rapidly taking over. There are also double-speed versions of 802.11b and 802.11g emerging, sometimes flagged with a '+' symbol.

Who needs cables? Take your laptop to the garden.

7

PART

PC maintenance

Computer hardware is a curious mix of solid-state components with no moving parts to break or seize and precision-engineered, finely-tuned devices that require regular maintenance and cleaning to work at their best. Things can and do go wrong, so here we consider some sensible preventative measures to stop potential problems in their tracks, some basic trouble-shooting techniques, and a maintenance regime designed to keep your PC running smoothly.

Windows utilities

As you may expect, Windows (95/98/Me/XP) comes equipped with an array of useful tools designed to optimise its performance. While many people swear by the likes of Norton SystemWorks or McAfee Office, others never spend a penny on third-party utility software. We'll consider commercial alternatives shortly but for now let's look at what Windows itself has to offer.

Defragmenting your hard disk improves performance.

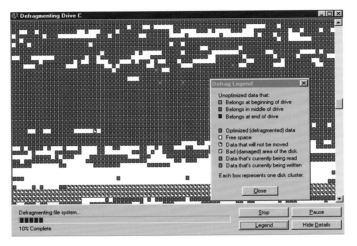

Disk Defragmenter

The data on your hard disk is stored in lots of small packets. Although this is an efficient use of space, one side effect is that individual files can get split apart and stored piecemeal all over the disk. This process is known as fragmentation and it only gets worse with time. Every time you open a fragmented file, Windows has to track down all the different bits and pieces and stick them back together again – a time-consuming and wasteful business. However, with a utility called Disk Defragmenter, you can restore all files to their former glory and buck up system performance at a stroke.

It's important to close down all system activity before you begin: any attempt by a program to write data to the hard disk causes Disk Defragmenter to start from scratch. Close all running programs, such as your word processor, browser or email program in the usual way, and disconnect from the internet. You should end with a clear Desktop and no buttons on the Taskbar. Then look at the System Tray – the part of the Taskbar next to the clock – for icons that show which programs are running in the background. Right-click each icon in turn and select Exit or Close. You should be left with just the clock and speaker icons.

Finally, press the Ctrl, Alt and Delete keys simultaneously. This reveals any other open, but hidden, applications. Highlight each item in turn – with the exception of Explorer and Systray – and select End Task.

Now click Start > Programs > Accessories > System Tools. Here you will find Disk Defragmenter. Start the program and select the drive you wish to optimise (usually the C: drive).

Close down all programs before running Disk Defragmenter.

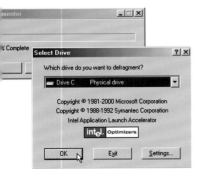

Tell the program which disk to work on.

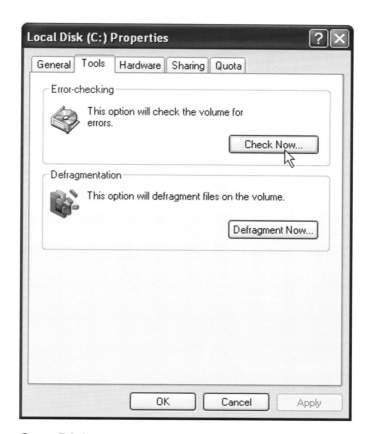

In Windows XP, the disk-checking utility is accessed by right-clicking a drive in My Computer.

ScanDisk

Whenever your PC crashes or closes down unexpectedly, you may notice that it runs through an error checking process next time you start it up. This is ScanDisk looking for, and hopefully fixing, file problems on the hard disk. However, you can also run ScanDisk on demand. Here's how.

In Windows 98/Me, click Start > Programs > Accessories > System Tools > ScanDisk. There are two options here: a Standard test, which is reasonably quick and checks all your files and folders for errors; and a Thorough test, which takes much longer but also examines the physical integrity of your hard disk. If you're having problems with your PC – perhaps a document won't open – the Standard test is usually enough, but we'd recommend a Thorough scan once in a while as part of a periodic system maintenance regime.

Check the box marked 'Automatically fix errors' to speed things up. You can set the parameters of what ScanDisk will and will not do in the Advanced dialogue box but the default options are just fine. As with Disk Defragmenter, leave ScanDisk to work in peace. If it finds any lost clusters (parts of files), it saves them with the extension .CHK in the root directory (the topmost folder in Windows). These may safely be deleted. If, however, ScanDisk reports any 'bad sectors', back-up your files immediately. Although Windows will not now write any new data to these unusable areas of the hard disk, it may be a sign of impending disk failure.

Windows XP operates slightly differently. Open My Computer to see your drives, then right-click the drive you want to check (usually C: drive). Select Properties from the menu, open the Tools tab and click the Check Now button.

Let ScanDisk automatically fix any problems it finds.

Disk Cleanup

Programs take up a lot of space but so can individual files, particularly web pages saved to the hard disk by your web browser. Disk Cleanup can automatically remove a good deal of this debris.

As with Disk Defragmenter and ScanDisk, Disk Cleanup is found in the System Tools menu. The program offers several options: simply check each box in turn for an explanation of what it does. Do be cautious about emptying the Recycle Bin, especially if you've just deleted a bunch of files. Sure as eggs is eggs you'll wish you hadn't permanently consigned that complete record of your household finances to oblivion three seconds after you push the button.

The Temporary Internet Files area may be quite large. This is your browser's cache – an area of your hard disk set aside for keeping copies of the web pages you visit. If you delete its contents, your browser will have to reload each page from scratch next time you revisit a favourite site instead of plucking some or all of its elements from the cache. This may slow down your surfing a little but the cache soon fills up again and the effects are short-lived. Besides, many web pages are updated frequently so having an old copy on your computer isn't really much of an advantage.

Disk Cleanup explains what it's going to do before it starts.

Maintenance Wizard

The problem with ScanDisk, Disk Defragmenter and Disk Cleanup is, of course, that you'll never remember to use them. That's why Windows includes Maintenance Wizard, a utility that lets you set up an automatic schedule for running one, two or all three programs at regular intervals. Once again, find it by clicking Start > Programs > Accessories > System Tools, and then run Maintenance Wizard in custom mode. Note that it's best to schedule these tasks to run at a time when you're not using your computer, like the middle of the night. You also have to ensure that no running programs will interfere with Disk Defragmenter (see above), so close down anything that's not absolutely essential and deactivate any screensaver before you bed down. Oh, and don't forget to leave your computer switched on and running.

Maintenance Wizard is not available in Windows XP.

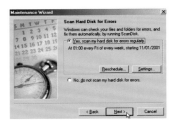

If you're prone to forgetfulness, what you want is a Wizard.

Registry Checker

The Registry is a database of Windows settings. Without the Registry, Windows won't start or run at all; and if the Registry gets corrupted, all manner of errors can crop up. It's well worth while making a manual backup of the Registry before undertaking any work on your computer, be it a new program installation or a hardware upgrade.

Click Start > Programs > Accessories > System Tools > System Information. Now click the Tools menu button and select Registry Checker. Accept the proposal to make a backup of the current Registry file.

Alternatively, in Windows Me and XP you can back up the Registry simply by making a System Restore point (see p153).

Registry Checker isn't available in Windows XP but only because XP includes some rather more robust tools that automatically protect the Registry from damage.

Add/Remove Programs

Ah, if only life was simple and you could install and delete software at will and with ease. Well, sometimes you can, but only sometimes. The trouble is that there's no single, catch-all, foolproof method for ridding a system of unwanted applications. Some come with their own uninstall utilities while others rely on Windows to do the work. Still others display a thoroughly leechlike determination never to be deleted.

One of the requirements for a product to carry the 'Designed for Windows 95' logo on the box is compliance with Microsoft's InstallShield standard. A 'true' Windows program should install smoothly and do away with itself just as easily. However, in practice, bits and pieces of programs are often left behind, notably empty folders and scattered cryptic files. Most worrying are orphaned entries in the Windows Registry, a record of all that makes your system tick. Conflicts and confusion in here can be serious. Windows XP controls rogue programs far more effectively than its predecessors, to the extent that it objects in the strongest possible terms if you try to install something that hasn't been tested and automatically backs up and restores any critical system files that are altered during installation or use.

But why bother getting shot of old software? Why not just let it be? Three reasons:

1 Old programs take up disk space. Sooner or later, you're liable to need it, so it's better to manage this as you go along

2 You might not realise it but many programs run continuously in the background even if you never actually use them to do anything useful. This eats into available RAM and has a detrimental effect on performance

3 Every additional program on your system increases the risk of conflict with another, more useful program. As a rule, tidy

Add/Remove Programs clear out the clutter. Unfortunately, it doesn't always work perfectly.

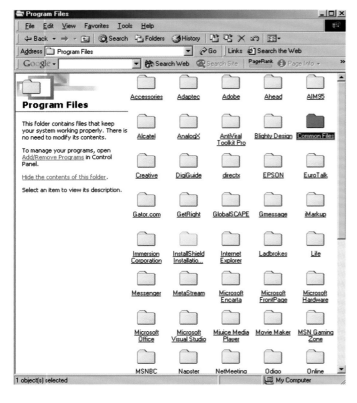

How many of your programs do
you actually use?

systems run more smoothly and you may find that simply
uninstalling some half-forgotten software miraculously cures no
end of unexplained ills.

So, click Start > Programs and see just what you've got onboard.
Point at any superfluous programs and see if an Uninstall option
appears. If so, select it and follow the step-by-step instructions. At
the end of the process, you may be warned that some elements of
the program must be manually removed. Make a note of any
details supplied. The leftovers are usually a top-level folder in the
Program Files menu and perhaps one or two sub-folders within.
Now click My Computer, select your hard disk, click Program Files
and find the folder(s) that you jotted down. These may now be
dragged straight to the Recycle Bin. Incidentally, Windows
Millennium Edition has the touching habit of refusing you access to
Program Files on pain of the sky falling in. Just override it.

Where a program doesn't come with its own uninstaller, click
Start > Settings > Control Panel > Add/Remove programs. This
brings up a list of programs that Windows can automatically
delete. Just highlight the program and click Add/Remove.

System Configuration Utility

You know the way that certain programs start automatically every
time you turn on your computer? This behaviour may be highly
desirable, as with anti-virus software, or may be intensely
irritating. To stop them in their tracks, there are three possibilities:

1 Look in the program's own Preferences or Options (or similar)
menu and see if you can uncheck a 'Start this program with
Windows' (or similar) option

2 Click Start > Programs and look in a folder called Startup. This
contains shortcuts to programs that start with Windows. To
remove a shortcut, right-click it and select Delete

3 If neither approach solves the problem of persistent programs,
click Start > Run and type 'msconfig'. Now click OK to launch
the System Configuration utility. In the Startup tab, you'll find a
list of programs and background utilities. Look for the offending
item and uncheck the box.

Nobble programs that start
without your permission with the
System Configuration utility.

Most well-behaved programs let
you decide when and whether
they start.

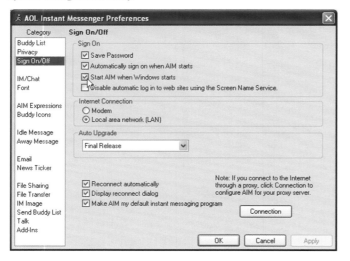

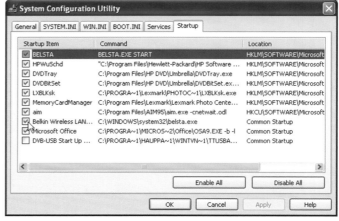

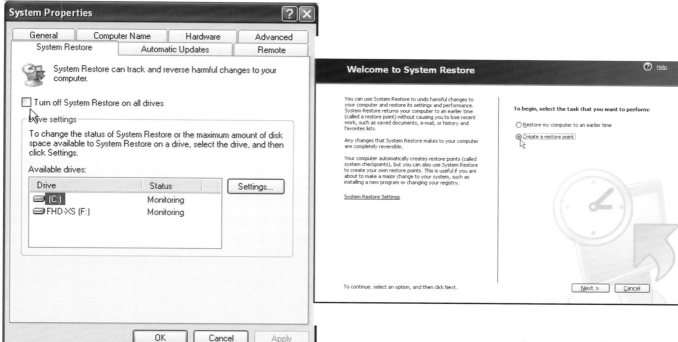

System Restore offers a 'get out of jail free' card.

System Restore

Windows Millennium Edition and XP include a background tool called System Restore. This takes regular 'snapshots' of the system and allows you to roll back in time in the event of trouble. For instance, if you install a rogue program and Windows starts crashing, you can restore your system to the way it was before the installation.

It sounds magical and, up to a point, it is. We'll mention it again in the trouble-shooting section but for now you should ensure that it's actually active.

In Windows XP, right-click the My Computer icon on your Desktop, select Properties and open the System Restore tab. In Windows Me, right-click the My Computer icon on your Desktop, select Properties, open the Performance tab, click File System and then click Troubleshooting. Here you'll find an option to disable the utility. Be sure not to.

You can make a manual checkpoint at any time, and we strongly suggest you do so before installing new software or hardware. Click Start > Programs > Accessories > System Tools and launch System Restore. Click the Create a Restore Point button and follow the directions. You can now revert to this checkpoint should anything go awry in the future (see p163).

Performance Options

Windows XP only, this one. As we've mentioned, Windows XP demands a fairly hefty hardware configuration to run smoothly. If your system is anywhere close to the minimum requirements – see p170 – you may see a considerable benefit by switching off some of the fancier display effects. Right-click the My Computer icon, select Properties, and open the Advanced tab. Now click the Settings button in the Performance section and check the Adjust for best performance option.

Bid farewell to fading menus and mouse shadows for a boost in raw performance.

PART **7** Third party utilities

The shelves of your local computer superstore are stacked with commercial utility software that promises to make amends for the failings of Windows and keep your PC running in tip-top condition for ever and a day. Bold claims indeed, and not wholly without merit. With all such packages, there is a significant overlap with Windows' own utilities and, in the case of the major suites, often some internal features overlap as well. But the real point of these programs is threefold:

1 Routine maintenance tasks like defragmenting a hard disk and trouble-shooting hardware conflicts are faster, more efficient and, above all, easier to manage than with Windows alone

2 You get value-added extra features into the bargain (see below)

3 Peace of mind. You don't have to be paranoid to believe that sooner or later your computer will self-destruct and take with it all your precious data, or that hackers will break into your system, steal your credit card number and make merry with your money. There's a good deal more hype than substance in these scare stories but the bottom line is that people feel safer with added security measures in place.

A utility suite reaches into Windows' darkest corners and the potential to do accidental damage should not be underestimated.

However, with power comes danger. Any utility suite has the potential to do enormous damage to your PC if handled incorrectly or unwisely. These are no empty words, incidentally: over the years, we've done almost as much harm as good with utility software.

Furthermore, utility software can slow your system down a tad during everyday operation. That's the trade-off for improved security and stability.

The big players in the utility software stakes are Symantec (**www.symantec.com**), McAfee, Inc (**www.mcafee.com/uk/**) and Iolo (**www.iolo.com**).

Trouble-shooting It's usual to find a 'one-click-solves-all-woes' button in utility suites, and certainly you can save a great deal of time and effort by letting smart software seek out and resolve your system conflicts. Hardware and software issues alike can be treated, including deep-rooted Windows problems.

Crash protection A utility that stops an impending crash in its tracks and gives you the chance to save your work is worth its weight in gold. Unfortunately, results tend to be variable.

Program uninstaller Dedicated program uninstallers that do a thorough job of deleting old software.

Zip utility What better way to save disk space and tidy up than by compressing multiple files into one much smaller file, called an 'archive'? Windows XP actually has zip-capability built in, so you can open existing zip files and make your own. Non-XP users can download the evaluation version of WinZip from **www.winzip.com**

Disk imaging This is the process of copying, or 'cloning', an entire hard disk in one move, up to and including the operating system, in

order to load it on another computer or to recover the current system in the event of a disaster. We discussed imaging back on p66.

Firewall A program that stops hackers from gaining access to your computer. Again, Windows XP has its own firewall but for everybody else this is an essential purchase. It's possible to buy products that bundle a firewall with anti-virus protection (see p156), which can save you money.

Encryption Want to keep your email or documents on your hard disk files secret? Then you'll be wanting a file encryption tool.

File recovery Deleted an important document by mistake? File recovery utilities can (sometimes) help.

File shredding Contrariwise, you might prefer that a deleted file is truly gone forever beyond all possibility or recovery. For this, you need a file shredder that overwrites the old file with binary gibberish – again and again and again.

Internet cleanup If you want to stop snoops checking up on your surfing, an internet trace eliminator is handy. Your computer has a sometimes unwelcome habit of keeping hidden records of all you do.

Password manager Rather useful, this one. You'll appreciate the importance of using secure passwords on the internet and are probably all too aware of the difficulty of remembering anything more secure than the dog's name. A password management utility can both create ultra-secure passwords for you and store them in a safe encrypted format.

Spyware This is software that sends your browsing history and other details to marketing companies that sell it on to advertisers who hope to target you personally. Deeply repugnant and something to be shot of. Spyware-blasting tools are often bundled with other utilities but you can also use Ad-aware (www.lavasoftusa.com) and Spybot-Search & Destroy (www.spybot.info). Both are free.

And then, of course, there's anti-virus software. But that, we strongly suggest – nay, insist – is not an optional extra. Read on…

See what's going on under the hood.

Programs keep crashing? Utility software can help save your work.

Many utilities do much the same as Windows, but usually rather better.

It's common practice for utility software to bundle multiple tools within a single screen.

PART

Viruses – a special case

However you cut it, computer viruses are a fact of life. At best, they're a hassle; at worst, downright destructive. You have to be something of a moron to release one 'into the wild', so to speak, but there's no shortage of them in the world. And so all we can do is accept that viruses are with us in abundance and take adequate precautions.

Update your anti-virus software frequently.

Protect and survive

Viruses are basically programs like any other. They typically have two parts: a means of getting into your system and a reason for doing so. Once inside, a successful virus might scramble your data, sit quietly in the background doing nothing at all until triggered by a key date, or instantly email copies of itself to everyone in your address book. Some viruses are created by geeks for the supposed kudos of being clever with code; others are written by malicious saboteurs bent on wreaking havoc across company networks or the internet itself. In all cases, your first and necessary line of defence is to install an anti-virus program. This attempts to identify inbound nasties in one or both of two ways: by spotting and isolating known viruses (highly effective but not much use against brand new bugs that aren't yet in its database); and by looking for suspiciously virus-like behaviour (a good safety net, although far from foolproof).

If you suspect you've been infected, scan your system without delay.

Moreover, because new viruses appear all the time, you must update your anti-virus program regularly. If it has an auto-update feature, all to the good: allow it to call home for updates whenever you're online. Otherwise, make it a point of principle to manually update it at least once a month, and preferably once a week. Some developers now release daily updates. Remember, an out-of-date anti-virus program is next to worthless, so don't assume that you're safe just because your new computer came with an anti-virus program pre-installed.

Get wise to hoaxes

Equally important is making sure that you don't contribute to the spread of these pests yourself. Never pass on a virus warning without first checking whether or not it's a hoax. If a rampant email virus can bring a network to a standstill, a flurry of hoax warnings is almost as damaging. So, if you get a virus warning in your email inbox, pause and consider before forwarding it to anybody else. Does it exhort you in the strongest possible terms to tell everybody you know 'WITHOUT DELAY!!!!'? Does it proclaim that unspeakable things will happen to your hard disk if you get infected? Does it read like the work of an idiot trying to get a rise out of the world? Then it's almost certainly a hoax. Check it out at Vmyths.com (**http://vmyths.com**) before you pass it on.

Don't be fooled by silly hoaxes – check them out on the web.

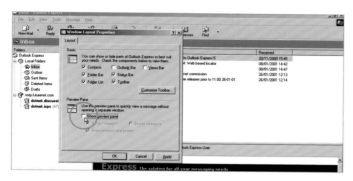

Switch off the Preview Pane option in your email program for better security.

Quite what pleasure virus writers derive from their dark art is a mystery.

Periodically check for Windows updates and install any security patches.

Sensible steps

Aside from installing and updating anti-virus software, there are various things you can do to minimise the risk of infection.

Switch on your anti-virus program's background scanning features to ensure that all files are checked at the point of being opened.

Check for security updates and patches for your email program. If you use Microsoft's Outlook or Outlook Express, go here:
http://windowsupdate.microsoft.com
(It will only work if you are using Internet Explorer version 5 or better.)

Don't download files from strangers on the internet and delete, without opening, any unasked for email attachments. Don't even sneak a peek at mystery messages in your email program's Preview Pane, as this alone can be enough to do the damage. For maximum security, switch off the Preview Pane option altogether. In Outlook Express, click Layout in the View menu and uncheck the Preview Pane option.

Be wary of Word documents (files with the extension .DOC) and Excel spreadsheets (extension .XLS), as these could harbour macro viruses.

Never open an executable file type unless and until you've scanned it for viruses *and* been personally assured by the sender that it's safe. Extensions to look out for include: .EXE, .VBS and .JS.

Don't beg, steal or borrow dodgy software.

Beware of files that try to hide their true extension e.g. BritneySpearsNaked.jpg.vbs. Many a mug would assume that this is a harmless image file but the .VBS extension gives the game away: it's a script virus.

PC MAINTENANCE
Taking precautions

A lightning strike could fry your computer – so better get protected!

A little foresight and rudimentary background knowledge about the various things that can harm a computer system goes a long way towards averting serious problems. We covered static electricity at the very outset and we'll take the liberty of assuming that you already know that water and electricity don't mix (i.e. don't play with your PC in the bath). Here are some other essentials.

Magnetism

If it wasn't for the magic of magnetism, your PC's hard disk couldn't permanently store data. Nor could floppy or Zip disks transfer files from here to there and back again. But while magnetism is undoubtedly a force for good, it can also do inordinate damage to your data when allowed to interfere with the strictly controlled conditions present in your computer system. It pays, therefore, to ensure that magnets in any form and data stored on magnetic media (as opposed to optical media like CD and DVD discs) do not come into contact with one another.

For instance, never stick a magnetic paper clip holder on your PC case lest it interfere with the workings of the hard disk. Keep floppies well away from magnetic sources like printers, fridges, cars, mobile phones, hi-fi speakers – and, of course, plain magnets. It's also unwise to stack them on top of the PC case. As we've mentioned before, a magnetic screwdriver may be perfect for retrieving lost screws but it shouldn't be allowed anywhere near the inside of a computer.

Power surges

You may well have a good idea of just how regular, or smooth, your electricity supply is. Then again, you may have no idea. Peaks and dips are sometimes made evident by an unexpected brightening or dimming of the lights, but a serious peak, or spike, can do a computer serious damage.

Now, all reputable PC manufacturers build some form of surge protection into the power supply controlling the current that flows into the system but it's unwise to rely on this alone. If you consider that you're at risk from sudden voltage spikes, or if you simply want an added layer of protection, consider a heavy-duty surge protector. This is a circuit breaker sited between your computer and the electricity supply that stops any spike in its tracks.

There are several different designs but the most effective deploy a metal-oxide varistor (MOV) that routes the surge straight to earth and thus out of harm's way. Unfortunately, these can be worn down over time and a single large surge may kill an MOV outright. This is fine – after all, it's the job of a surge protector to take the bullet for your computer – but, rather bizarrely, some units don't actually tell you when the MOV is dead. To avoid an unwarranted sense of security, be certain to buy a surge protector with a warning light that clearly displays whether or not it's working!

A surge protector prevents sudden spikes in current – or lightning strikes – from reaching and potentially destroying your hardware. This model sits under the monitor.

Power cuts

Spikes aren't the only power problem to afflict the computer user. Who hasn't experienced a sudden power cut and lost a minute, an hour or a day's work in a flash? Such incidents generally prove a great crash course in the importance of saving your work regularly as you go along but it's a lesson we could all do without. The answer is to invest in an uninterruptible power supply (UPS) of some sort. A UPS is essentially a battery unit that draws its charge from the mains supply and takes over power supply duties the instant a power outage occurs. Different models offer different levels of protection – some may provide only a few minutes power while others can keep a PC running for an hour or two (plenty of time to leap out of bed in the middle of the night, drive to the office and salvage that vital company backup job) – but the principle is simply to give you sufficient time to save your work and close down the computer in an orderly manner.

A backup battery lets you carry on working in the event of a power failure.

PART  **Trouble-shooting**

Although it's certainly true that your computer system is on a fast-track to obsolescence almost as soon as you get it home from the store, the good news is that hardware reliability these days is generally very high. Today's inkjet printer should still be technically capable of churning out full colour pages long after the manufacturer stops making the ink cartridges it requires. Also, most problems are evident immediately rather than, say, six months down the line. A new processor either works or doesn't work: it doesn't 'sort of work'. (For just this reason, incidentally, an expensive extended warranty is usually a waste of money.) You may be lucky and never experience a hardware problem; then again, your shiny new PC may be dead on arrival. Here we look at how to begin the trouble-shooting process.

PART

Trouble-shooting in general

The first and entirely natural reaction to a computer problem is often one of panic, compounded by the realisation that we haven't been quite as rigorous with our backing up regime as we might have been. What happens if it never works again? Have all our files and documents disappeared forever? It's at such moments that we wish that we had taken a college course in advanced computing and that we had never become so reliant upon the infernal contraption in the first place.

Checklist

It's obviously beyond the scope of this book to cover every eventuality – which is why we wrote the *Haynes Computer Troubleshooting Manual* – but here are some general approaches that just might resolve your woes. First off, though, just relax. Put the kettle on. Go for a walk or sleep on it. Then calmly, rationally and logically think through the problem. Computers are fantastically complex at heart but also ridiculously simple in the sense that one bit plugs into another and can be easily replaced.

1 Are your PC and all its peripherals plugged in and switched on? How about any switches on the cases – could these have been inadvertently knocked to the off position? Be sure to check the power supply too – could a fuse have blown somewhere, either in the main fuse box or in the device's

Updated drivers can cure many known problems so check the manufacturer's website.

own plug? Perhaps your surge protector has given up the ghost and cut the power as a safety precaution? If your USB mouse, keyboard, printer or whatever are connected to a hub, try connecting them one at a time to a USB port on the computer itself to establish whether the hub is at fault. Many a call to technical support – and a resulting red face – could have been spared by these simplest of all checks.

2　Check that all cables are in place. It may mean crawling around behind your system but it's not uncommon for a USB cable to fall out of its socket and render a device inoperative. Cables themselves can also fail, albeit rarely, so it's well worth while experimenting with a spare cable before assuming that a device is a dud.

3　When did your PC or the suspect peripheral last work without trouble? Can you undo any changes that you've made in the meantime? Hardware conflicts (see Techie Corner on p169) are common and temporarily uninstalling a newly-connected component can often fix a problem or at least pinpoint its probable cause. Poorly written software applications are also notorious for thoroughly confounding the most carefully arranged system settings, so uninstall any recent additions (see p151).

4　If you're running Windows Millennium Edition or XP, try the System Restore utility. This is a way of reverting the computer's configuration settings to an earlier, trouble-free time. Click Start > Programs > Accessories > System Tools > System Restore and check to see when Windows made its last 'checkpoint'. Roll back to this checkpoint and see if the problem goes away. If so, all you have to do is work out what you did in the interim to cause all the bother. If not, try an earlier checkpoint. Don't worry about your files and documents, incidentally, as these are unaffected by System Restore.

5　 If your computer won't start normally, try starting it in Safe Mode instead. This loads and runs a bare-bones versions of Windows in which many features are unavailable, but it gives you a chance to carry out repair work (including running System Restore, uninstalling software and carrying out a virus sweep). To access Safe Mode, press the F8 key while the computer is starting.

System Restore can take you back in time to a point before your troubles began.

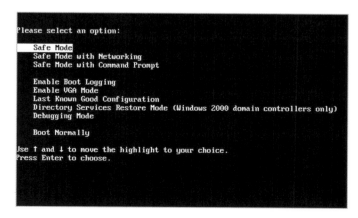

Safe Mode lets you troubleshoot Windows from within.

6 Also check Device Manager (p23-24) for clues about any troublesome hardware. A device with a problem will be flagged with a yellow exclamation mark. Try removing any such device from the system. If the problem goes away, reinstall it. If the problem comes back, replace the device.

7 When Windows won't start at all, even in Safe Mode, try booting the computer from a start-up floppy disc or a bootable CD-ROM (such as the Windows XP disc). If you can do this, you can be fairly sure that the problem lies with Windows, not your hardware. Now would be a very good time to check that you have backups of all your important files, for the next step is not to be taken lightly: reinstalling Windows. You can either perform an over-the-top installation, in which Windows is reinstalled over the existing copy (and your files and folders should be preserved unharmed); or a clean installation, in which Windows is installed afresh (and all existing data, including your files and folders, is deleted in the process).

8 If you took our advice earlier and you make regular images of your hard disk, you could try restoring the most recent image file now. This works like the ultimate System Restore, as it replaces your current hard disk with an exact copy of the way it looked at the time the image was created. Be careful, though. Restoring an image file completely overwrites your current version of Windows and all your file and folders, so you lose any files created between the time of the image and the present. It is therefore vital to back up such files onto recordable CD or any other removable media now. You should also consider that an image won't get you out of a hardware problem. If your computer keeps crashing or refuses to boot because the memory is faulty, restoring an image will have zero impact. Finally, while restoring a disk image may be one way of curing a virus infection, there is a possibility that the virus will attack the image file itself during restoration. In the worst case, this could wipe out your healthy disk image as well as your infected Windows installation. Our advice is to rid yourself of the virus first. Visit any of the anti-virus companies' websites for advice.

9 If a specific device is at fault, don't forget to read the manual. There's no better place to find specific help, and you'd be surprised at just how many potential problems are unique to one particular peripheral. In these cost-conscious days, chances are that the full manual (as opposed to that wafer thin 'quick installation guide' that fell out of the box) is an electronic file rather than a proper printed affair. It may have been installed on your PC when you first loaded the software or you may have to find it on the installation CD-ROM.

10 Also visit the manufacturer's website and look for a Support or FAQ (Frequently Asked Questions) page. You may even find a discussion forum where you can search for similar issues and/or post a personal request for help. Quite possibly,

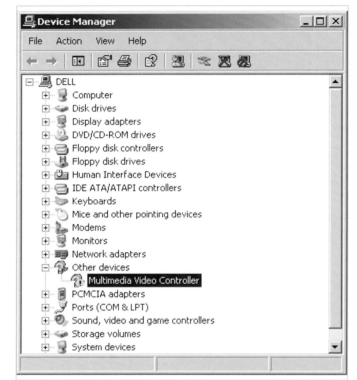

Suspect hardware is flagged in Device Manager.

the fault that you're currently experiencing is well known and a cure is already on hand in the form of a downloadable software 'patch' or bug-fixer. You'd think they'd tell you about this, would you not, especially if you registered your product when you first acquired it, but we've lost track and count of important – even essential – bug fixes slipped quietly onto support websites without any fanfare whatsoever. Of course, this assumes that your computer itself is working and has an internet connection, or that you have access to a working machine.

11 In a similar vein, try searching the web at large for help. For instance, enter a few relevant keywords into a search engine like Google (**www.google.com**). This is particularly helpful if the computer keeps freezing and throws up a 'fatal exception' or 'stop' error (the so-called Blue Screen of Death), in which case you should search for the error description or reference number. Newsgroups are also a fabulous resource. The easiest way to access and search them is again via Google: go to **http://groups.google.com** and search away.

12 If the problem is related even tangentially to Windows or another Microsoft product, you might find the answer you need in the Microsoft Knowledge Base (**http://support.microsoft.com**). This is a massive, searchable online database of questions and answers. Again, type in a couple of keywords and see what you get. As with any search, results are best when you provide accurate, pertinent information, such as the text of an error message.

13 To identify or eliminate a problem with a hardware device, the most effective procedure is one of substitution. If your keyboard should die, say, your first question would be: which is at fault – the keyboard itself or the interface on the computer? To find out, plug in a working keyboard or experiment with the malfunctioning keyboard on another computer, or, preferably, do both. The same applies to any peripheral, from the monitor to the mouse or a printer or scanner.

14 Where it gets slightly tricky is with internal components, particularly when the cause is not evident or if the computer won't start at all, as it's not so easy to whip out a hard drive or processor and test it out elsewhere. Even here, though, there are things you can do. The key is stripping the system down progressively until you reach the point where it works. Observing all the usual safety precautions (p33), proceed as follows:

a) Check that all internal cables are in place and firmly connected. Pay special attention to the processor fan's cable connection to the motherboard.

b) If you have more than one memory module, remove all but the module in the DIMM 1 slot. Restart the computer. If that doesn't do the trick, replace the module in DIMM 1 with one of the others, and try again.

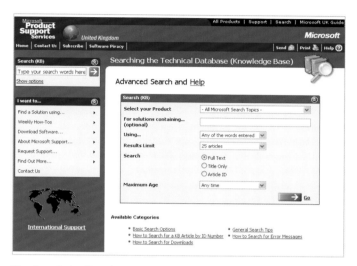

The Knowledge Base is an invaluable one-stop shop for help.

c) Remove the sound card and any other expansion cards with the sole exception of the graphics cards. This eliminates any possible short circuits. If the computer now works normally, replace each card one at a time until you identify the culprit. Obviously – at least we hope it's obvious – you must turn off and unplug the computer between each operation.

d) If it still won't start, disconnect the floppy and CD/DVD drives from the motherboard and unplug their power cables. Leave only the hard drive connected (and double-check its power connections).

e) Still no go? Swap the hard disk's ribbon cable with another and try again.

At this point, if the computer still refuses to start, you have either a broken PSU or motherboard, or dead memory modules or hard disk drive. Further elimination testing is required to definitely establish the problem. However, if you have access to another PC, try removing the hard disk from the faulty machine and installing it temporarily as a secondary (slave) device in the working system. This way, you can test whether the drive itself is functional and, if so, copy all your files and folders to the primary drive or to some form of removable media.

PART 8

Trouble-shooting specific problems

It's obviously beyond this manual's scope to cover every hardware eventuality. Indeed, it's beyond the scope of *any* manual, even those daunting 1,000+ page tomes that claim to teach you how to build a PC from scratch (but not necessarily how to switch it on). However, here are a handful of the more common problems to afflict the average computer system.

Hard disk

Insufficient disk space If Windows tells you that there's insufficient disk space to complete an operation or to save a file, you need to clear out some clutter sharpish. See p.151 for tips on uninstalling old software and making more space. Better still, pre-empt the problem now. Click My Computer, right-click on C: drive, and select Properties. If the disk is more than 75% full, it's time to start making economies.

Permanently busy If your hard disk appears to be permanently busy (lots of whirring noise and a constantly blinking light on the PC's case), chances are you don't have enough system memory and Windows is using the disk as a RAM substitute. Add more memory (see p.38).

Unexpected disk noises may be a sign of impending failure. Backup your work onto removable media (recordable CDs, Zip disks, a tape drive or similar) immediately *before* switching off your PC, and seek professional advice.

Optical drives

Disc won't eject? Restart the PC and try again. If the tray still won't open, *switch off the power*, flatten out a paperclip and poke it into the small hole on the drive's case to release the mechanism.

Problem CDs If one particular CD won't work properly, perhaps sticking during playback or freezing the system, try cleaning it with a soft cloth. If it's scratched, it's probably irreparable, although it's certainly worth trying to run it in somebody else's computer before giving up hope. If, however, you start experiencing problems with many or all your CDs, the drive itself has a problem. Buy a lens cleaning disc to shift internal dust.

Suddenly no sound from your audio or multimedia CDs? Check the PC's volume settings are not muted (double-click the loudspeaker icon near the clock in the Windows System Tray and/or run any sound card diagnostic software). If this doesn't work, the audio cable connecting the drive to the sound card has probably become detached. Open up the case (after taking all the usual precautions – see p.33) and reattach it.

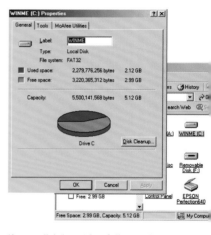

If your disk is getting full, now is the time to start making economies.

Turn to your sound card's diagnostic utilities to trouble-shoot audio problems.

Set the refresh rate as high as your graphics card and monitor will allow.

DVD disc won't play? Check that it has the same regional code as your DVD drive (see p.79). Windows itself can't play DVD movies so you need a DVD player program. Is this installed?

Monitors

Unusual patches of colour on the screen, especially near the edges, are probably due to some magnetic influence. Use the degauss button or software utility to remove excess magnetism and move any magnetic sources – including speakers and the PC case itself – further from the monitor.

Flickering If you can see any flickering in the screen image, the refresh rate is too low. This way lies headaches and a most uncomfortable user experience. See p.115 and make sure that the refresh rate is set to at least 72Hz (or higher if your monitor supports it).

TECHIE CORNER

Disk disaster
Hard disks don't go on for ever (although most are still spinning quite happily come the time for an upgrade) but, short of a catastrophe like complete destruction or theft, it's almost always possible to recover data from a badly damaged disk. Many companies worldwide specialise in data recovery, and some will even attempt a diagnosis through a modem link. The problem is that it's always an expensive option. That's why it pays to archive your old data on Zip disks or recordable CDs or similar.

However, if you simply must recover current data, the procedure depends upon the severity of the problem. If you've accidentally deleted the odd file or reformatted an entire disk and now wish you hadn't, or if a virus wreaked havoc, specialist software alone can sometimes recover your data. In the case of physical damage, a disk that's still working from an electro-mechanical point of view – i.e. still spinning – is relatively easy to work with, but even a device badly damaged by a power surge or fire can sometimes be persuaded to yield usable data. Not one to try at home you understand: call in the experts.

Modern printers typically have a host of configurable options.

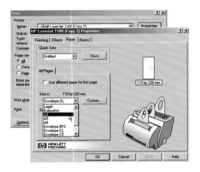

Are paper size and layout settings correct?

Games and other software can play havoc with your display settings so go back to basics. Click Start, point to Settings, click Control Panel, and then double-click Display to access the options.

Printers

Poor print quality? This could be down to your choice of paper or some problem with the software settings. Experiment with different paper types and weights and be sure to run any diagnostic program that came with your printer. Also try printing at different resolutions.

Toner If your laser printer's toner is almost exhausted, remove the cartridges and rock it gently from side to side. This re-distributes the remaining toner and may see you through until you can buy a refill. Note that shaking an inkjet's ink cartridges does no good whatsoever.
  Inkjet cartridges can move fractionally out of the correct alignment, leading to blurred, bleeding or fuzzy prints. Run the appropriate software utility to fix this.

Blurrred Is what you see on screen most definitely *not* what you get on paper? Check that the correct paper size is selected in the print setup settings and be sure to select portrait or landscape views as appropriate.

Paper jams are less common these days than once they were but can still stop a printer dead, particularly if you use a paper type or weight that the printer is not designed to accommodate. Consult the manual for instructions on how to open the unit and extract the mangled sheets.

Modems

Connection Can you hear your modem in action as it dials up your Internet Service Provider (ISP)? Adjust the volume control on an external model until you can hear it chirruping when it tries to make a connection. For an internal modem, click Start > Settings > Control Panel > Modems and adjust the volume in the Properties section of the General tab. So long as you can hear *something*, the modem's not entirely lifeless and the problem is likely to be with the telephone line or, more commonly, a temporary hitch with the ISP.

Has your modem suddenly stopped working? If you've recently added a new extension handset or fax machine somewhere in your house, there may now be too many devices trying to share the same line. Try temporarily unplugging any additions and see if your modem comes back to life.

Diagnostics Try running the Windows diagnostic utility. Click Start > Settings > Control Panel > Modems and select the Diagnostics tab. Highlight your modem and click More Info. Windows now tries to contact the modem and reports back with any problems. 'Port already open' is the most common error message, and invariably means that some software application – perhaps a fax of voice-mail program – is messing up the settings. Close down all running programs and try again.

Pump up the volume to hear if your modem's alive or dead.

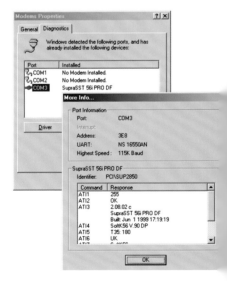

Windows will have a stab at rooting out modem troubles.

Are you connected If you *think* that you're online but can't access any websites or send and receive email, make sure that you're really connected. Click Start, click Run, type 'winipcfg' (without the quotes), and hit Enter. If you see an IP Address that's not just a string of zeroes, you are indeed online and it's likely that the problem is a blip with your ISP. If not, your modem is failing to connect. For serious diagnostics, look here (and yes, this does rather presuppose that you can get online, in which case why do you need a modem trouble-shooter?):
http://support.microsoft.com/default.aspx?scid=kb;EN-US;q142730

An IP address is a guarantee that you're online.

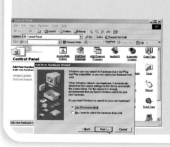

TECHIE CORNER

IRQ-some When hardware devices talk to the rest of the computer, they use one, more or none of the following: Interrupt Request (IRQ), Input/Output address (I/O), Direct Memory Access (DMA) and Memory Address. The first of these, IRQ, frequently leads to conflicts where two devices fight over access to the processor and system resources. Thankfully, Windows can configure most modern 'Plug-and-Play' devices (including *all* PCI expansion cards) automatically, but older ISA expansion cards may have jumpers that need to be set correctly.

In the event of a hardware conflict (warning signs: a new peripheral device or expansion card doesn't work or Windows starts freezing and/or crashing inexplicably), get along to Device Manager and look for evidence.
Click Start
Click Settings
Click Control Panel
Click System
Click the Device Manager tab.
Expand the list of hardware by

clicking the + signs and look for anything marked with a (!) — an indication that Windows suspects a problem. Highlight any such devices and click Properties for details.

The most common state of affairs is when two devices try to share a single IRQ. Windows will then prompt you to (temporarily) disable one in order to use the other. This very rapidly becomes a pain, so a better solution by far is to reassign their IRQ addresses. Sounds complicated? Not really — but the precise solution depends on the specific problem. Note too that Windows can share a single IRQ address between certain devices, so just because two bits of hardware have the same IRQ doesn't necessarily mean that you need to fiddle unless one or the other doesn't work or there's a (!) warning in Device Manager.
Look here for a detailed exposition of IRQ and its system stablemates:
http://www.pcguide.com/ref/ mbsys/res

PART

Windows XP: the cure for all ills?

Microsoft's latest operating system for PCs, Windows XP, has been widely heralded as its most stable platform yet, and our experience bears this out. But it's not exactly a no-brainer upgrade option.

Here, for instance, are the stated minimum system requirements for the Home version of XP:

● Pentium II 233MHz processor

● 128MB RAM

● 1.5GB free hard disk space

Hefty stuff, and this really is the absolute minimum that you'll need for a happy relationship with XP: it runs a lot more smoothly with a 600MHz-plus processor and 256MB RAM under the hood.

XP comes pre-installed on (virtually) all new PCs these days but we'd hesitate to recommend it as an upgrade unless you're confident that your system can cope. Also, because XP doesn't support all older hardware, you may find that you can't get a suitable driver for your creaky printer or peripherals. Some software may also refuse to work.

For absolute peace of mind, download and run Microsoft's Upgrade Advisor, a tool that scans your PC and reports back with any potential problems. Unfortunately, it's a 50MB(!) download, which makes it impractical unless you have a high-speed broadband internet connection. You can get Upgrade Advisor here: **www.microsoft.com/windowsxp/home/howtobuy/upgrading/advisor.asp**

Alternatively, try the Windows Catalog tool on Microsoft's website. This lets you check your hardware and software piece by piece for XP compatibility: **www.microsoft.com/windowsxp/home/howtobuy/upgrading/checkcompat.asp**

If in any doubt, follow our advice on p69 and install XP in a separate hard disk partition.

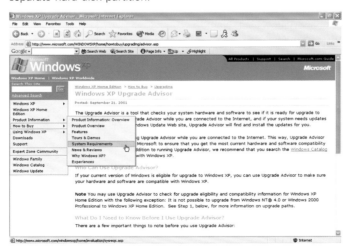

Windows XP is the best operating system around but don't consider it unless your PC is up to speed

No more crash and burn

If Windows XP is indeed for you, improved reliability is the welcome result. At the simplest level, because XP is better at predicting and averting impending trouble, this means far fewer computer crashes. Wisely, XP stops dodgy third-party software from mucking up its settings in the first place and, should one application freeze during use, it's usually possible to close it and carry on without rebooting the computer. Like Millennium Edition, XP includes the System Restore utility which takes regular snapshots of the computer's configuration settings and lets you revert to an earlier point should anything suddenly go awry. The Help and Support centre includes some useful step-by-step diagnostics, and there's a one-click link to the Windows Update website where you can keep your PC current with essential patches and bug fixes.

Windows XP also includes a very useful driver rollback feature. If you upgrade a device driver and it creates problems – a not uncommon occurrence – you can easily revert to the previous driver. Access this feature via Device Manager (see p24).

Another nice addition is the Last Known Good Configuration start-up option. This restores the Windows Registry to a previous version that worked. It operates in a similar manner to System Restore but is fully automatic and can be accessed from the Safe Mode start-up menu (i.e. when you hit F8 to stop Windows loading normally).

Recovery Console

And then there is Recovery Console, a powerful but awkward fix-it utility that you can only access by booting from the Windows XP installation CD-ROM (or from downloadable XP start-up disks: see p84).

Assuming that the BIOS is configured to boot from the CD drive, place the Windows XP CD-ROM in its drive and restart your computer. You'll be prompted to press any key to continue, which is an apt moment to recall the hapless consumer who called a £1.50/minute help-line to ask where the Any key was on the keyboard. Three options appear: install Windows (which we'll come back to in a while); repair the existing copy; or quit. Press R to do the second of these.

You now have to choose which copy of Windows you want to work with, but this is only of concern in a multi-boot environment. If you only have one copy of Windows installed, type 1. Finally, enter your password, if you normally use one to log into Windows.

You can use Recovery Console to replace damaged system files, which is a useful way of repairing a corrupt copy of Windows without going through a full reinstall. You can also run XP's version of Scan Disk from here and potentially restore the Master Boot Record. However, Recovery Console is a text-only command-driven utility and not to be taken lightly. You'll have virtually no chance of achieving anything useful until you bone up a bit on how it works. Here are a couple of useful links:

http://support.microsoft.com/default.aspx?scid=kb;EN-US;314058
www.wown.com/j_helmig/wxprcons.htm

Get out of a hardware jam fast with Roll Back Driver.

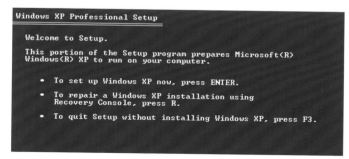

Select Last Known Good Configuration when booting from the Windows XP CD and you might – just might – recover from trouble seamlessly.

Press R to start Recovery Console or Enter to install Windows.

No point-and-click ease of use with the powerful but obtuse Recovery Console.

An over-the-top reinstallation of Windows XP can keep you running

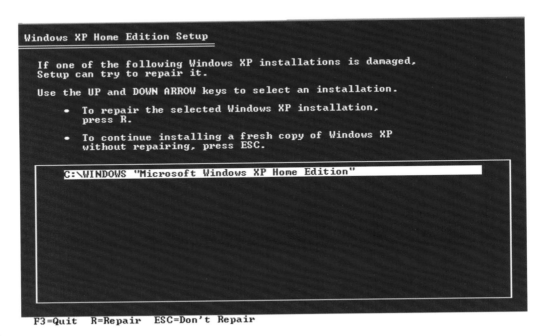

```
Windows XP Home Edition Setup

If one of the following Windows XP installations is damaged,
Setup can try to repair it.

Use the UP and DOWN ARROW keys to select an installation.

    • To repair the selected Windows XP installation,
      press R.

    • To continue installing a fresh copy of Windows XP
      without repairing, press ESC.

┌──────────────────────────────────────────────────────────────┐
│ C:\WINDOWS "Microsoft Windows XP Home Edition"                 │
│                                                                │
│                                                                │
│                                                                │
└──────────────────────────────────────────────────────────────┘

F3=Quit   R=Repair   ESC=Don't Repair
```

Don't forget to activate the Windows XP firewall immediately after a repair installation – and before going online for the first time.

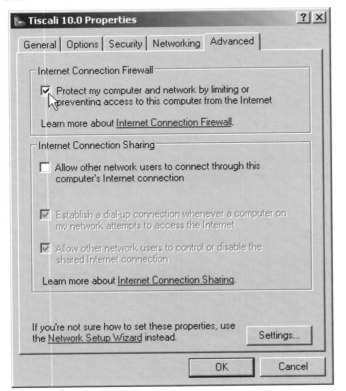

Reinstalling Windows

Returning to the Windows XP boot menu, the first option invites you to install Windows. If Recovery Console hasn't helped, your best bet now would be to reinstall Windows over the top of the existing version. This should not affect your files and folders, although that can't be guaranteed (which is why a current backup is so essential).

If you proceed here, the Windows setup routine initially looks like it's about to start a fresh installation, which would wipe out everything. Presently, though, you'll be given an option to repair the current installation. Be sure to press R at this point. Windows will reinstall itself and, hopefully, repair any damaged system files in the process.

But one big word of warning: you will now have to reinstall any Windows patches and service packs, and you should do so very quickly indeed to minimise the risk of picking up a virus or a worm. First, switch on the Windows XP firewall. Click Start > Connect To and right-click the icon that represents your internet connection. Select Properties from the popup menu, open the Advanced tab, and check the Internet Connection Firewall box. Now take your computer online and update it at the Windows Update site (click Start > All programs > Windows Update). Be sure to download all critical updates. As we write, all historical updates have just been amalgamated in a super-update called Service Pack 2.

Virtual help

Perhaps the most innovative feature in XP goes by the name of Remote Assistance. The idea is simply this: many, perhaps most, PC problems can be quite easily fixed by somebody who knows what they're doing, so why send your computer back to the store for repair when you can get instant help from a clued-up colleague, friend or family member? With Remote Assistance, you invite another XP user to access your computer remotely over the internet (or local network), whereupon they can control your mouse and keyboard and work with your PC just as if they were sitting beside you at your desk.

The system works strictly by invitation only – i.e. it's up to you to initiate the help session by inviting somebody you trust to come onboard and take control – so there's no danger of hackers breaking in, fiddling around and stealing your files. With the right help at the other end of your internet connection, the end result can and should be a computer that's up and running again in no time.

The ultimate hands-on trouble-shooter? It's certainly a welcome step in the right direction.

Thanks to its Windows 2000 Professional heritage, the bottom line is that XP has superior trouble-shooting tools to any other version of Windows, while being more resilient and resistant to damage in the first place.

Keep your computer trouble-free with automatic updates.

When all else fails, invite an expert to fix your computer over the internet with XP's Remote Assistance.

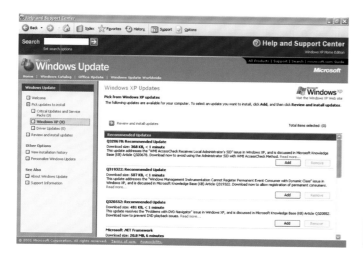

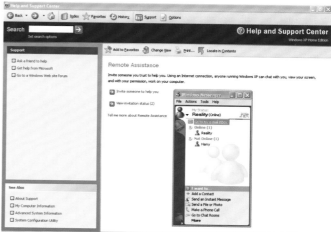

9

PART 9

COMPUTER MANUAL

Appendices

Appendix 1
BIOS and CMOS

Two more dread acronyms!

BIOS (Basic Input/Output System)

This is usually found in the shape of a chip on the motherboard. BIOS kicks in when you first start your PC to get the essential parts of the system – keyboard, monitor, hard disk, ports and so on – up and running before (and independently of) the operating system. Modern BIOSs are Plug-and-Play, which means that they can automatically recognise and configure most new expansion cards and hardware devices. They tend also to be flash-upgradeable – i.e. they can be updated via an internet download. The historical trouble with BIOS is that pre-1994 versions couldn't recognise hard disks larger than 528MB; pre-1996 versions managed no more than 2.1GB; and more recent chips gave up at 8.4GB. The good news is that special software (usually supplied with large hard disk drives) can circumvent these infuriating limitations. However, a flash upgrade or even a replacement chip is a better long-term option. If your computer was made by a major manufacturer like Compaq or Dell, you should be able to download a BIOS upgrade from the Support section of the manufacturer's website. With smaller PC brands, however, you'll have to find out who made your PC's BIOS. Look for the name during the start-up process – probably Award, Phoenix or AMI – or follow this procedure:

 Start

 Settings

 Control Panel

 System

 the Device Manager tab.

Now click the Print button, select System Summary, and click OK. At the very top of the first page to be printed you'll find the BIOS details.

A Device Manager report reveals who made your BIOS. Check the manufacturer's website for further details.

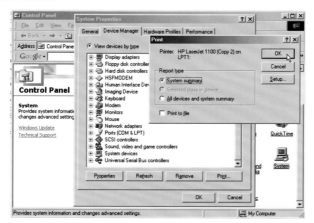

Changing the boot order

You can use the BIOS setup program to determine certain key system settings, including which drive the computer boots from first. Ordinarily, BIOS is set up to check the floppy drive for a bootable disk – i.e., a disk containing a program that can start the computer – and, if it finds nothing, to boot Windows from the hard disk (C: drive). This is exactly the arrangement that you want, as it lets you start the computer with a start-up disk (see p26-28) in the event that there is a problem with Windows.

However, you may want to start the computer with a bootable CD-ROM instead, particularly if you want to install Windows XP on a new hard disk or work with the XP Recovery Console. To do this, you must configure BIOS to check the CD (or DVD) drive before booting from, or attempting to boot from, the hard disk.

To get to the BIOS setup program, restart the computer and press the F1, F2 or Delete keys while it is running through its self-checking routine. Check the motherboard or PC manual for details of which key is required. One of the opening screens may say 'Press DEL to run Setup', in which case take that as your cue. Otherwise, just keep pressing those keys until the BIOS menu appears.

Once in BIOS setup, you need to find the boot order priority menu and move the CD drive higher in the priority list than the hard disk. All BIOS menus are controlled by the keyboard alone, not the mouse, but you should find an explanatory guide to navigation at the bottom of each screen. Change the boot order to floppy drive first, followed by CD drive, and finally hard drive. You now have the option of booting from a floppy disk or CD at any time.

Once you have reordered the boot list, be sure to save your changes when you exit the setup routine. This usually means pressing the F10 key but, again, help is provided on screen.

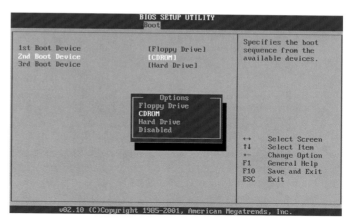

Shuffle the CD drive up the priority list if you need to start the computer from a bootable CD-ROM.

CMOS (Complementary Metal-Oxide Semiconductor)

This is essentially a form of permanent memory, powered by a battery, which keeps a record of your system's configuration when the power is off. Here you might change details about, for instance, the drive order in which your PC tries to boot (usually floppy drive followed by the hard disk), power management settings, port configuration and BIOS settings.

Doesn't sound like much fun, does it? Truth to tell, you might never need to go near the CMOS. However, should the motherboard battery fail or something else go seriously awry, a permanent record of your CMOS setup would prove invaluable. Now would be a very good time indeed to make just such a document.

You can access the CMOS records through the BIOS setup routine just described. Go to the CMOS menus and write down everything you see, especially material pertaining to the computer's disk drives, like capacity, cylinders, heads, landing zone (don't ask), sectors and all the rest. When you're through, press the Escape key until you're back at the start page, and confirm that you want to exit without making any changes. Windows will now start as normal.

For more on this stuff, check the excellent BIOS survival guide here: **http://burks.bton.ac.uk/burks/pcinfo/hardware/bios_sg/bios_sg.htm**

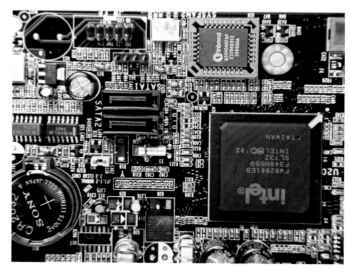

The circular battery on the motherboard (lower left corner) means that CMOS retains its memory when the mains power is off.

Appendix 2
Guide to connectors

PS2 ports and plugs.

Serial port and plug.

Parallel port and plug.

Too many holes and don't know how to fill them? Here's a quick guide to common computer connectors.

USB ports and plug.

Firewire port and plug.

RJ-45 port and plug.

3.5mm ports and plug.

VGA port and plug.

RJ-11 port and plug.

S-video port and plug.

DVI port and plug.

SPDIF port and plug.

Composite video port and plug (yellow) plus stereo audio (red and white).

UHF/VHF port and plug.

Name	Connects what?
PS/2	Mouse and keyboard
Serial	Mouse (old-style), modem or handheld electronic PDA/organiser
Parallel	Printer and sometimes a scanner
USB (Universal Serial Bus)	Pretty much all new peripherals that once used the slower serial or parallel connectors
FireWire (or IEEE 1394)	External drives. Also ideal for connecting digital camcorders
RJ-45 (Ethernet)	Computer to a network
3.5mm	Speakers and microphone
VGA (Video Graphics Array)	Monitor
RJ-11	Modem to the telephone line
S-video TV-out	Computer to TV set (very high image quality)
DVI (Digital Visual Interface)	Digital monitor
SPDIF (Sony/Philips Digital Interface)	Speakers or external audio decoder. This is an optical interface
Composite audio/video	Computer to TV set (high image quality). A separate stereo audio signal is transferred through the red and white cables
UHF/VHF (Ultra/Very High Frequency) TV-in	A standard rooftop aerial for TV reception on the PC

Appendix 3
Installing a new motherboard

A new motherboard is the ultimate computer repair, or upgrade, or both. The motherboard lies at the heart of the computer. Indeed, it is the computer. Everything else, from the processor to memory to the hard disk to the monitor, is an accessory, and a replaceable accessory at that.

A new motherboard is a fearsome thing to contemplate, right? Actually, wrong. Installing one is easy. The trick is buying the right one.

We've looked already at swapping one sound or video card for another, changing the hard drive and adding an extra slice of memory. Finally, we must consider the business of changing the motherboard itself. Why would you want to do such a thing?

● **You want a faster computer.** The two primary ways to speed up a slow system are with a memory and/or processor upgrade. As we've said, memory matters more. However, there may come a point where an extra memory module just won't suffice, particularly if you're running on an old (and hard to get hold of) format. A processor upgrade will improve performance to a degree but you may find that your motherboard doesn't support a faster chip than the one that's currently installed. It certainly won't support a shift from, say, a Pentium III to a Pentium 4 on account of the different slot and socket designs.

● **You want to play computer games or work with digital video.** The bottleneck here would be the graphics card. If your motherboard lacks an AGP slot, upgrading to a more powerful graphics card will be limited to a PCI model, and that's a severe restriction. Even if you do have AGP, you can't use a fast 8x-speed card in a 2x or 4x-speed slot.

● **The motherboard is broken.** Motherboard failure does happen, although relatively rarely. With the best will in the world, you increase the risk of damage every time you open the case covers or perform minor internal surgery. Indeed, we recently fried a motherboard (that's fried as in rising smoke!) during a routine processor replacement. We never found out what went wrong, but there's the rub: it's far, far easier to replace a dead component, even a motherboard, than attempting to diagnose and repair a serious problem.

In each case, you needn't necessarily buy a new computer to achieve your goal. Remember, PCs are modular. If you want to change or upgrade component A, there's every chance that components B, C and D are still perfectly functional. Even with a new motherboard, you can reuse much of what remains.

Here are the most likely candidates:

Case So long as the new motherboard fits the old case, as it will if you stick with the industry-standard ATX design, you can simply rebuild your new system in the old case.

Sound card You would want to chuck out an old ISA sound card but any PCI version will fit your new motherboard. Besides which, you may prefer the simplicity of a motherboard with integrated multi-channel audio (we certainly would).

Graphics card As indicated above, this really depends whether your old card is an AGP model, whether it's compatible with your new motherboard (see especially the voltage concerns on p91), and whether you're content with its performance. Again though, you may opt for integrated (AGP) graphics, in which case you won't need your old card.

Hard disk Should be no problem. A faster or bigger disk may be desirable but the old one will work just fine. The one exception would be if you buy a motherboard with Serial ATA sockets only. For maximum compatibility, seek out a model with SATA and IDE/ATA sockets.

Network, modem, USB, FireWire and other expansion cards Anything PCI-flavoured will transfer across just fine.

Monitor, keyboard and mouse Plug them in and use them as before.

And those less likely:

● **Processor** For reasons stated, you can only replace like for like. In the best case, your old motherboard might have a Socket 478 interface with an early Celeron or P4 processor installed. Chances are – but check the manual first – that you could reuse this processor in your new Socket 478 motherboard. However, it's more likely that a PC in need of a motherboard upgrade or repair has an earlier Pentium II or III (or AMD Athlon equivalent) chip onboard, in which case you'll certainly need a new processor. This shouldn't prove too onerous: the very latest processors always cost a fortune but anything just slightly past its peak will be more than capable and surprisingly cheap.

● **Memory** Again, your old memory probably uses an outmoded design or runs at an incompatible speed. We would always advise that you buy new memory modules when installing a new motherboard.

● **Power Supply Unit** An important consideration. There are actually two potential problems here. First, if you have been systematically upgrading your computer or intend to do so now, your old PSU may be a touch underpowered to run the whole show. A 300 watt PSU is really the minimum you should have in a Pentium 4-class computer. Check the old PSU casing for details of its power output.

Secondly, and more importantly, you will certainly need to replace the PSU if your system currently has an AMD Athlon processor and you're moving to an Intel Pentium motherboard. This is because Pentium 4 motherboards have an additional power connector (called ATX 12V) and only a P4-compliant PSU has the requisite cable. In fact, this may also apply if you're moving from a Pentium II or III system. Just to be awkward, AMD stipulates that any PSU designed for use in an Athlon-based system should have its cooling fans arranged in a particular way.

The bottom line is thus that you may well need to replace the PSU at the same time as your motherboard. Not that this is a bad thing, as such, for you should get years of trouble-free service from a fresh device, but it is something to be aware of (and budget for).

On a related note, you should also check whether a potential motherboard requires a third power connection known as ATX Auxiliary. If it does, you need a PSU with the requisite cable.

Main power *A standard design compatible with all ATX motherboards.*

ATX Auxiliary *Uncommon, but you'll need a PSU with this cable if the motherboard has an ATX Auxiliary socket.*

ATX 12V *Required by all Pentium 4 motherboards. Don't reuse your old PSU with a P4 system unless it has this cable.*

5.25-inch drive *This plug powers the hard drive and CD/DVD drives.*

3.5-inch drive *This plug powers the floppy drive (and/or a media card reader).*

Input/output panels

The procedure for installing a new motherboard is essentially straightforward. Industry standards like the ATX form factor mean that any compatible motherboard will fit in any compatible case, and your drives and expansion cards can be easily reconnected. The only slightly fiddly part is whipping out the old input/output panel faceplate and installing its replacement. So a word about that now.

All motherboards provide a built-in range of inputs and outputs. How many you get depends on how many features are integrated within the motherboard itself rather than provided by additional expansion cards. The recent trend has been heavily towards integration, with the result that today's motherboards typically have many more inputs and outputs than yesterday's. But in order to ensure compatibility with computer cases, these sockets are all located in the same corner of the motherboard and are arranged in a panel of fixed dimensions. This panel fits a hole in the case, and so the inputs and outputs can be accessed externally.

Because designs vary so widely, all new motherboards are supplied with an input/output panel template. This must be installed in the case first in order that the sockets can poke through – and this in turn means removing the old template first.

One other factor to be aware of are the motherboard standoffs. Rather than attaching directly to the case, motherboards are screwed into little raised pillars called standoffs that attach to pre-drilled holes in the case (and vary significantly in design and method). When you remove the old motherboard, the standoffs should stay in place. However, while the ATX form factor guarantees that the case will have standoff positions to match the holes in your new motherboard, there is no cast-iron guarantee that the existing standoffs will all be in the right position, particularly if you're installing a smaller (but still ATX-compliant) motherboard than the one you're removing (as, in fact, is the case in our worked example). This means that you may need to move a few standoffs around before you can install the new motherboard. A minor hassle, but don't skimp it: the last thing you want is a motherboard that's not properly supported for want of a standoff in the right position.

Three motherboards from different eras but each is compliant with the ATX form factor. This means that their input/output panels will fit the same hole in any ATX case. The wide variations in socket layouts highlights the importance of input/output templates.

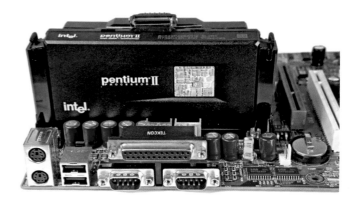

Installing a motherboard

Here, we remove an old slot-based motherboard and replace it
with a Socket 478 (Pentium 4) model.

*Before commencing any internal work on your PC, re-read the
safety precautions on p33.*

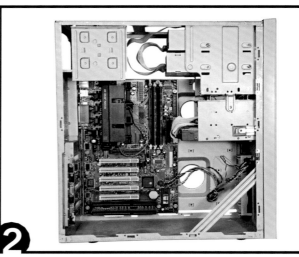

*Strip the motherboard clean by unplugging all drive cables and
power cables and removing all expansion cards. This is also the
time to remove the Power Supply Unit itself if you have to
replace it. You should end up with a motherboard that is no
longer connected to the computer in any way. However, there is
no need to remove the processor or memory modules. If you
intend to reuse them, they can be more easily removed when
the motherboard is outside the case. Here, we have still to
unplug the cables running to the front case buttons (bottom
right) but everything else has been stripped.*

*Unscrew the motherboard from the case (or, more correctly, from
the case standoffs). You'll find screws around the edges of the
motherboard, in the corners, and also one or two dotted around
the middle. Be sure to get them all. Now remove the
motherboard from the case. You may have to tug a bit to free it
from the input/output panel.*

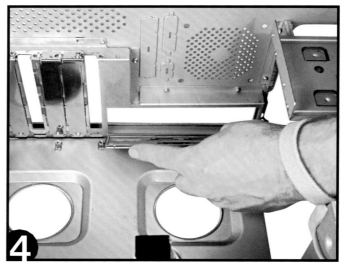

*Remove the old input/output panel template. Some clip in and
out of place; some slide; some screw. Install the new template
panel according to the directions. Be sure to get it the right way
round. The side with the two round holes for the PS/2 mouse
and keyboard connections will be adjacent to the power supply.*

5 Here we can see the motherboard standoffs still in place. Carefully remove your new motherboard from its anti-static bag and, holding it only by the edges, match its drill-holes with the standoff positions. If necessary, move the standoffs around until you have a perfect match. You might prefer to remove them altogether and start afresh with the standoffs supplied with your new motherboard. Either way, you must have a standoff in the correct position for every drill-hole in the motherboard.

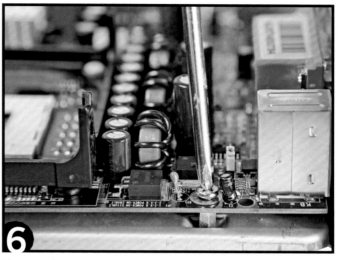

6 Very carefully install the motherboard in the case and screw it to the standoffs. Do not over-tighten the screws as it's possible to distort or even crack the motherboard with excessive force (yes, that's experience talking again).

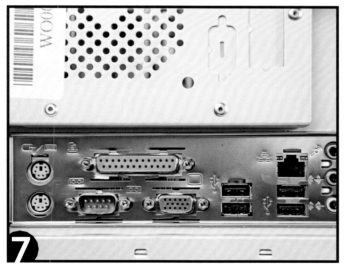

7 The tricky bit with a motherboard installation, as you'll now have discovered, is matching the inputs and outputs with the template. Sometimes, it seems they just don't want to mesh, but mesh they will in the end. It's a two-handed job, or better still two person. Here we see the end result: lots of lovely sockets perfectly aligned with holes in the template.

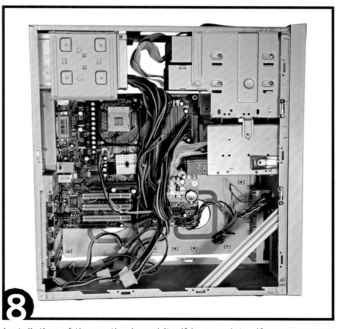

8 Installation of the motherboard itself is complete. If you compare this shot with Step 2, you'll see the difference in motherboard size. This new version is smaller but considerably more adept. We have also installed the replacement P4-compliant PSU and made that all-important ATX 12V cable connection. All that remains is to install a processor and heatsink/fan and a memory module or two, reconnect the drives and plug in all the old expansion cards. Oh, and put the case covers back on.

PART 8

APPENDICES

Appendix 4
Alternatives to upgrading

Although we are all in favour of computer upgrades – which is handy given the nature of this book – our enthusiasm is tempered with a concern for avoiding needless expense and hassle. All too often, people are persuaded to part with their cash for swanky new software that they don't really need – and then forced to upgrade their hardware because that swanky new software demands a supercomputer spec.

Consider, for instance, the minimum system requirements (and we stress the word minimum) for Windows XP:

- 300 MHz processor
- 128MB RAM
- 1.5GB free hard disk space.

No problem at all there for any new PC and most older models can be brought up to speed with a memory upgrade and/or a larger hard disk. But with only 128MB RAM onboard, Windows XP is relatively sluggish to begin with. Once you start multitasking – i.e. running two or more programs or processes – everything slows rather rapidly.

In contrast, Windows 98 Second Edition ran (and still runs) on a mere 16MB or 32MB of RAM and about 150MB of hard disk space.

There may be good or even compelling reasons to upgrade to Windows XP – better stability, much improved support for external devices like MP3 players, and the bald fact that some new software will only run on XP – but a Windows upgrade should always be a balanced decision. Remember, despite Microsoft's marketing practices, an operating system is fundamentally a framework on which you build by adding your

Freeware and shareware aplenty at Download.com and others like it.

⑤ WHAT'S NEW IN SOFTWARE		MORE DOWNLOADS

Lantern 3.0
Shine a light into the depths of your network with this management package. In addition to giving you a detailed overview of your infrastructure, Lantern lets you seamlessly collaborate and share files.

- AppRocket 1.2
- BearShare 4.5
- 3D Canvas 6.5.0.5
- AcePlayer 1.09

▸ New Releases
▸ **Most Popular**
▸ Top Rated
▸ Mac Software
▸ Power Downloader

Audio & Video
MP3 Search · Burners · Players · Rippers · Video...

Internet
Tools · Privacy · Pop-Up Blockers · Chat · Browsers...

Games
Retail Demos · Action · Strategy · Arcade · Cards...

Business
E-mail · Spam Filters · Finance · Applications...

IS/IT
Remote Access · Sales · Internet Operations...

Mobile
Palm OS · Pocket PC · Cell phone · Wireless Utilities...

Design Tools
Image Editing · Flash Tools · Digital Photo · Authoring...

Web Developer
HTML Editors · Site Management · PHP · Flash Tools...

Software Developer
Tools & Editors · Java · ActiveX · XML · Flash Tools...

Utilities & Drivers
Drivers · Antivirus · File Compression · Security...

Desktop Enhancements
Screensavers · Desktop Management · Themes...

Home & Education
Calendars · Language · Music · Teaching Tools...

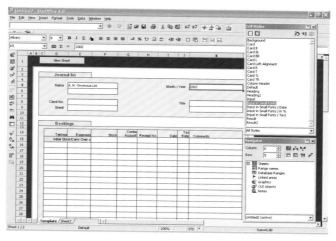

own applications and fine-tuning the computer to do what you require of it. An upgrade that slows down your computer is hardly for the best. Moreover, you may find that your older programs and, in particular, games simply won't work with XP.

One option is maintaining a Windows 98 installation in a separate hard disk partition (see p69 for details). The point here is that you can keep your familiar undemanding operating system and related software while simultaneously upgrading to Windows XP. Just boot into Windows 98 whenever you want a fast working environment that's unencumbered by XP's heavy-duty system requirements.

Low-spec software

Consider the system requirements for these three office suites:

	Processor	Memory	Hard disk space
Microsoft Office 2003 (**www.microsoft.com/uk/office**)	233MHz	128MB	260MB
Open Office (**www.openoffice.org**)	Any Pentium	64MB	250MB
Ability Office (**www.uk.ability.com**)	Any Pentium	32MB	50MB

Now, it is not for us to say here which office suite we think is best (although we might point out that one is free, one is cheap, and one costs an absolute fortune), but merely to point out that the average user can probably get by perfectly well with, say, Ability Office on a relatively low-spec machine.

We heartily recommend that you consider alternatives to big brand software in every department, particularly if your hardware has been round a few blocks. You may well find that you can get a small, specific program that does precisely what you want without straining your system or bloating your hard disk with features and options that you'll never go near. You might even get it for free, such is the popularity of freeware (yours to keep) and shareware (yours to try before you buy) software. Have a browse through the likes of Download.com (**www.download.com**), Tucows (**www.tucows.com**) and Top Shareware (**www.topshareware.com**).

The latest software may sport 9,999 fancy features but it won't do your sums any faster or write your words for you; and just because a shrink-wrapped box bears a name that you recognise doesn't mean that the software inside is any better written or less buggy than an equivalent program produced by an enthusiast with a focus more on the needs of the end user than the bottom line.

PART 9 Appendix 5 Glossary

Here's an at-a-glance guide to many of the techie terms used throughout this manual, along with several more that you'll doubtless come across on your travels around the mind-numbing world of computer jargon. Always remember this: if in doubt about what something means, just ask (at which point you'll invariably find that the salesperson, who is so keen to take your money, doesn't really have a clue either).

Let's start with a table of the storage units used in computer-speak.

Name	Symbol	Size
Bit	b	A single binary unit (i.e. a 1 or a 0)
Byte	B	8 bits
Kilobit	Kb	1,024 bits (= 128 bytes)
Kilobyte	KB	1,024 bytes
Megabit	Mb	1,048,576 bits (= 131,072 bytes)
Megabyte	MB	1,048,576 bytes (= 1,024 kilobytes)
Gigabyte	GB	1,073,741,824 bytes (= 1,024 megabytes)

286/386/486 Early processors from Intel used to power desktop computers and superseded by the Pentium processor

56,000bps/56Kbps The theoretical top speed of modern modems (i.e. capable of receiving up to 56,000 bits of data per second)

512,000bps/512Kbps The accepted norm for a broadband internet connection, just under ten times faster than a modem connection

ADF Automatic Document Feeder. An attachment for scanners and printers that enables multiple sheets to be processed without manual intervention

ADSL Asymmetric Digital Subscriber Line. A broadband internet service that uses the existing copper wire telephone network

AGP Accelerated Graphics Port. A computer interface (usually a slot on the motherboard) designed for a high-performance graphics display

AMD Advanced Micro Devices. A manufacturer of computer processors and related hardware

Analogue A continuous signal

Anti-virus software A program designed to protect a computer from malicious viruses

ATAPI Advanced Technology Attachment Packet Interface. An interface for connecting disk drives to a computer

Athlon A family of powerful processors developed by AMD

ATX An industry-standard form factor (size and shape) for computer motherboards and cases

Backup A copy of vital computer files made for safekeeping

Bandwidth A measure of how much data can be transferred at any one time

BIOS Basic Input/Output System. Software stored in a chip that controls the operation of a computer at its most fundamental level

Blanking plates Removable covers on a computer case that protect unused expansion slots

Bluetooth A wireless networking technology

Boot To start a computer from a floppy disk, a CD or the hard disk

Broadband A high-speed internet connection service

Bus A path on a motherboard through which data can pass

C

CD-ROM A version of the compact disc that holds computer Data; CD-R (Recordable) and CD-RW (Rewritable) formats are blank discs on which files may be saved with a CD writer driver

Celeron A slower but cheaper version of the Pentium processor

Chipset Integrated circuits on the motherboard that provide support for the microprocessor, memory and expansion slots

Clock speed The rate at which a computer's processor operates, expressed in megaHertz or gigaHertz

CMOS Complementary Metal-Oxide Semiconductor. A chip that remembers basic system settings

Colour depth A measure of how many colours a monitor can display: 1-bit colour is black and white; 24-bit colour is up to 16.7 million distinct hues

COM port Communications port. A connector for devices such as printers and modems

Composite video A method of transferring a video signal from one device to another, commonly used to connect computers to television sets

Control panel An area in Windows where you can configure your PC

CPU Central Processing Unit. The main system processor

Crash When the computer goes wrong and stops working!

CRT Cathode Ray Tube. The glass tube used to produce an image in a television set and computer monitor (uses an electron gun to stimulate a phosphorous coating on the screen)

Cursor An arrow on the screen controlled by the mouse, or an insertion point in a document

d

Data Binary information

Default An action performed automatically in the absence of any alternative instruction

Defragment To reorganise files that have become split up and are stored piecemeal on the hard disk

Desktop The main screen within Windows before you launch any programs, home to icons such as My Computer and the Recycle Bin

Dial-up Networking The program Windows uses to connect a computer to the internet through a phone line

Digital In contrast to analogue, a digital signal is composed of discrete packets of information (basically, a series of on/off signals)

DOS Disk Operating System. A text-based operating system for PCs developed by Microsoft, the precursor to Windows

Dot pitch The distance between the tiny dots on a monitor screen that together make up a picture

Download The process of acquiring a file on to your PC from the internet

DPI Dots Per Inch. A measure of an image's resolution: the higher the DPI, the greater the clarity

Drive A machine that reads data from and writes data to a disk

Drive bay A space in a computer reserved for a drive

Driver A software program that lets the operating system 'talk' to and control a device

DSL Digital Subscriber Line. A technology that offers high-speed internet connections over standard copper telephone lines. The common UK version is Asymmetric DSL (ADSL), which allows more data to be downloaded than uploaded

Duron A slower but cheaper version of the Athlon processor

DVD Digital Versatile Disc. A type of compact disc capable of storing a huge amount of data, including movies. There are currently three families of recordable DVD drives: DVD-R/RW, DVD+R/RW and DVD-RAM

DVI Digital Visual Interface. An interface used to connect digital monitors to computers

e

EPP Enhanced Parallel Port. The modern, fast version of the parallel port used to connect a printer (a replacement for the slower Centronics standard)

ESD Electrostatic discharge. Static electricity, potentially fatal for computer components

Ethernet A technology that enables several computers to be connected together in a network

Expansion card A circuit board that can be added to a computer to enhance its capabilities

Expansion slot An interface on a motherboard used to connect an expansion card

FAT File Allocation Table. A cataloguing system that records where every file is stored on a hard disk

Firewall A program that aims to protect a computer against unauthorised access, particularly by hackers

FireWire (also known as IEEE 1394 and i.LINK). A high-speed interface with which devices can be connected to a computer

Flatbed A type of scanner that uses a flat glass plate, much like a photocopier

Floppy disk A non-floppy plastic square that holds up to 1.44MB of data (okay, it's floppy on the inside!)

Format To format a disk is to make it useable in a certain type of drive

Full duplex The ability to send and receive data simultaneously

GPU Graphics Processing Unit. A processor integrated on a graphics card with the purpose of producing 3-D and other video effects

Graphics card (sometimes called a video card) The circuitry in a computer that controls the monitor display, usually in the form of an expansion card

Hard disk A magnetic disk on which may be stored a great deal of data, including a computer's operating system

Hardware The physical components that make up a computer system

Hub A device that sits between other devices and provides a common connection point, typically in a network

Icon A small clickable image that denotes a file or application within Windows

IDE/ATA Integrated Drive Electronics/Advanced Technology Attachment. The interface used to connect hard disk drives to the computer's motherboard

Inkjet printer A device that squirts wet ink on to paper in order to print text and images

Intel A manufacturer of computer processors and related hardware

Interface The look and feel of a software program; or the means by which computer components communicate

IRQ Interrupt Request. One of the means by which hardware devices gain the processor's attention

ISA Industry Standard Architecture. The oldest type of expansion slot still found in PCs

Jaz drive A high-capacity storage device made by Iomega

Joystick A device for controlling the action in computer games

Jumper Small pins that control the settings on drives and motherboards

Laser printer A device that uses dry toner and laser light to print text and images

LCD Liquid Crystal Display. The technology used in flat-panel monitors whereby liquid crystal is charged with an electric current

Memory card A small, solid-state (no moving parts) chunk of memory used to store photos and/or data in portable devices such as digital cameras and handheld computers

MIDI Musical Instrument Digital Interface. A means of connecting electronic musical instruments to a computer

Modem A device that enables a computer to use the telephone line in order to communicate with other computers in a network, especially the internet

Motherboard The central circuit board in a computer to which all other devices are attached

Multimedia Loosely speaking, a combination of text, sound and video. Most CD-ROMs are multimedia, as are many websites

Network An arrangement of two or more connected computers in which they have shared access to resources like folders, printers and the internet

NIC Network Interface Card. An expansion card that enables a computer to join a network

Notebook A portable computer. Used to be called a laptop. Still is by some

NTFS New Technology File System The successor to FAT

OEM Original Equipment Manufacturer. This refers to computer components sold directly and exclusively to manufacturers (i.e. not available to the public)

Operating system Software that governs the workings of a computer, both in terms of hardware and applications

Optical disc A storage medium such as a CD or DVD from which data is read by a laser

Partition A sub-division of a hard disk that the computer treats just like a separate hard disk

PCI Peripheral Component Interconnect. An expansion slot standard, faster and more flexible than ISA

Pentium A family of powerful processors developed by Intel

Pin 1 A method of ensuring that computer cables are connected correctly, involving colour-coding on the cable and an identifying mark on the device and connector

Pixel The smallest single point on a display screen. At a screen resolution of 1,024 x 768, the full image is made up of 786,432 pixels

Plug-and-Play A standard that enables a Windows-based PC automatically to recognise and configure any new device

Port An external socket used to connect devices to a computer

Processor A silicon chip that processes data. Effectively, your PC's brain

Program A set of instructions that enables a computer to perform certain tasks. One example is a word processor

PS/2 A round 6-pin interface used to connect mice and keyboards to a computer

PSU Power Supply Unit. A unit that plugs into the mains electricity and supplies a computer's motherboard and drives with the current they require to operate

QWERTY The standard layout of the keys on a computer keyboard, where the first 6 letters on the top row are Q,W,E,R,T and Y

RAM Random Access Memory. Dynamic memory used by a PC as its working space

Registry Windows' database with information on all hardware and software that together comprises the PC system

Resolution A measure of the level of detail in an image on either a monitor screen or printed page

RF Radio Frequency. A wireless technology used to connect peripheral devices such as keyboard and mice without the use of cables

ROM Read Only Memory. As in a BIOS chip or CD-ROM, this is a form of memory used for data storage that can be accessed (read) but not changed (written)

Router A network device that controls the flow of data among connected computers

SATA Serial ATA A new serial (as opposed to parallel) interface for connecting hard disk drives to a computer. Unlike IDE/ATA, each SATA channel supports only one drive. SATA allows for much faster data transfers between the drive and the motherboard

Scanner A device that uses a light sensor to convert printed documents into data which can then be interpreted by software on a computer

SCSI Small Computer System Interface. A fast interface used to connect devices to a computer

Serial port A port on the back of a PC used to connect devices such as mice and modems

Software Computer programs, including application software, such as a spreadsheet program, and operating systems, such as Windows

SPDIF Sony/Philips Digital Interface. A digital audio interface that can be either an electronic plug and socket arrangement (typically using a 1/8-inch jack called phono or RCA) or a fibre-optic cable in which the signal is transmitted optically (i.e. with light)

S-video A method of transferring a video signal from one device to another, commonly used to connect computers to television sets; S-video generally offers better quality than composite video

Swap file An area of the hard disk used by Windows as 'virtual memory', or surrogate RAM

Taskbar A bar running along the bottom of the screen in Windows that shows a button for each program that is running

TFT Thin Film Transistor. A method of controlling an LCD display by means of transistors

TWAIN The software interface standard that enables scanners to work with imaging software

USB Universal Serial Bus. A relatively fast interface with which peripherals can easily connect to a computer

Upgrade To improve, enhance or modify the performance of your computer

Utility A software program designed to offer useful extra features or to automate routine tasks

V.90/V.92 Communications standards that modern modems adhere to

VGA Video Graphics Array. A basic standard governing monitor displays (16 colours at a resolution of 640 x 480)

Video card See graphics card

Virus A malicious computer program, usually spread on disk or over the internet

Virus writer A berk

Webcam A (usually low resolution) video camera that connects to a computer and lets you send live video images over the internet

Wi-Fi Wireless Fidelity. A radio frequency networking technology that works without direct cable connections

WYSIWYG What You See Is What You Get. This means that the image you see on your monitor is exactly what comes out of your printer

Zip drive A high-capacity storage device made by Iomega

Index

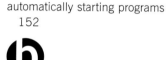

ACKNOWLEDGEMENTS

The author would like to thank John Sabine and Jon Sayers for their invaluable technical expertise. He would particularly like to thank Harry Sabbers, reformed geek, for his unwavering practical and moral support.

Author	**Kyle MacRae**
Technical Editors, UK	**John Sabine, Jon Sayers**
Technical consultant	**Jonathan Edgington**
Design	**Simon Larkin**
Page build	**James Robertson**
Photography	**Paul Tanswell, Tom Bain and Iain McLean**
Illustrations	**Matthew Marke**
Project Manager	**Louise McIntyre**